Quick-Guides to Inclusion 2

Quick-Guides to Inclusion 2

Ideas for Educating
Students with Disabilities

edited by

Michael F. Giangreco, Ph.D.
University of Vermont
Burlington

with contributions by

Lia Cravedi-Cheng, M.A.
Ruth E. Dennis, Ed.D., OTR
Janet M. Duncan, Ph.D.
Katharine S. Furney, Ed.D.
Patricia A. Prelock, Ph.D.
George B. Salembier, Ed.D.
Richard Schattman, Ed.D.
and
Alice Udvari-Solner, Ph.D.

·P A U L·H·
BROOKES
PUBLISHING Cọ

Baltimore • London • Toronto • Sydney

Paul H. Brookes Publishing Co.
Post Office Box 10624
Baltimore, Maryland 21285-0624

www.pbrookes.com

Typeset by PRO-Image Corporation, York, Pennsylvania.
Manufactured in the United States of America by
Versa Press, East Peoria, Illinois.

All royalties from the sale of this book are donated to nonprofit groups or agencies that meet human needs.

The individuals and situations described in this book are completely fictional or are based on composites of various people and circumstances, in which cases pseudonyms have been used. Any similarity to actual individuals or circumstances is coincidental, and no implications should be inferred.

Gender specifications used in this volume alternate throughout the text.

Library of Congress Cataloging-in-Publication Data

Quick-Guides to Inclusion: Ideas for educating students with disabilities/editor, Michael F. Giangreco;
   with contributions by Barbara J. Ayres . . . [et al.].
      p.   cm.
   Includes bibliographical references.
   ISBN 1-55766-303-3
   ISBN 1-55766-335-1
   1. Inclusive education—United States. 2. Handicapped students—Education—United States.
I. Giangreco, Michael F., 1956–   . II. Ayres, Barbara.
LC1201.Q53   1997
371.9′046—dc20
                                                      97-7106

British Library Cataloguing in Publication data are available from the British Library.

Contents

1. As a Team, Discuss and Plan Curriculum Together
2. Decide as a Team What "Curriculum" Means
3. Create a Student-Centered Curriculum
4. Get to Know Your Students' Abilities and Interests, and Use Their Expertise
5. Develop a Range of Multilevel Learning Outcomes for Each Student
6. Translate Multilevel Goals into Curriculum
7. Design Learning Experiences to Reflect Multilevel Goals
8. Adapt Instructional Approaches to Promote Active Learning
9. Look for Other Ways to Adapt Your Classroom
10. Don't Stop Now—Do it Again Next Year!

1. Know Each Student's Characteristics and Learning Styles
2. Choose Meaningful Learning Outcomes
3. Establish Shared Expectations
4. Use Good Teaching Methods
5. Use More Good Teaching Methods
6. Use Even More Good Teaching Methods
7. Plan How to Address Learning Outcomes in Classroom Activities
8. Provide Sufficient Learning Opportunities, and Be Consistent
9. Collect Data on Student Learning
10. Use Data to Make Instructional Decisions

1. Learn About Each Student's Preferred Communication
2. Provide Each Student with the Necessary Supports to Communicate
3. Create a Communication-Friendly Environment
4. Make Sure Each Student Has a Way to Communicate at All Times

About the Editor

Michael F. Giangreco, Ph.D., Research Associate Professor, Department of Education, University Affiliated Program of Vermont, University of Vermont, 499C Waterman Building, Burlington, Vermont 05405

Michael F. Giangreco has spent more than 20 years working with children and adults in a variety of capacities including special education teacher, community residence counselor, camp counselor, school administrator, educational consultant, university teacher, and researcher. Dr. Giangreco received a bachelor's degree from the State University of New York–College at Buffalo and graduate degrees from the University of Vermont and the University of Virginia. He received his doctoral degree from Syracuse University and has been a faculty member at the University of Vermont since 1988.

His work and educational experiences have led Dr. Giangreco to focus his research, training, and other work activities on three interrelated aspects of educating students with and without disabilities in their local general education schools: 1) individualized curriculum planning, 2) adapting curriculum and instruction, and 3) coordinating support services in schools. Dr. Giangreco is the author of numerous professional publications, including *Choosing Outcomes and Accommodations for Children (COACH): A Guide to Educational Planning for Students with Disabilities, Second Edition,* with Chigee J. Cloninger and Virginia Salce Iverson (Paul H. Brookes Publishing Co., 1998); the first set of Quick-Guides, *Quick-Guides to Inclusion: Ideas for Educating Students with Disabilities* (Paul H. Brookes Publishing Co., 1997); and *Vermont Interdependent Services Team Approach (VISTA): A Guide to Coordinating Educational Support Services* (Paul H. Brookes Publishing Co., 1996). In 1998, he collaborated with artist Kevin Ruelle to complete an unusual project called *Ants in His Pants: Absurdities and Realities of Special Education,* a set of 110 educational cartoons. He is a frequent presenter of educational issues and strategies. Based at the College of Education and Social Services and the University Affiliated Program of Vermont, he has applied his work in numerous schools across North America. His work has been advanced by the feedback and input of innumerable students (with and without disabilities), parents, teachers, administrators, related services providers, and other colleagues.

Contributors

Lia Cravedi-Cheng, M.A.
Lecturer
Department of Education
College of Education and Social
  Services
University of Vermont
453 Waterman Building
Burlington, Vermont 05405

Ruth E. Dennis, Ed.D., OTR
Research Assistant Professor
Department of Education
University Affiliated Program of
  Vermont
University of Vermont
499C Waterman Building
Burlington, Vermont 05405

Janet M. Duncan, Ph.D.
Assistant Professor
Department of Education
LeMoyne College
Syracuse, New York 13214

Katharine S. Furney, Ed.D.
Research Assistant Professor
Department of Education
College of Education and Social
  Services
University of Vermont
453 Waterman Building
Burlington, Vermont 05405

Patricia A. Prelock, Ph.D.
Research Associate Professor
Department of Communication
  Science and Disorders
University of Vermont
Pomeroy Hall
489 Main Street
Burlington, Vermont 05405

George B. Salembier, Ed.D.
Assistant Professor
University of Vermont
446 Waterman Building
Burlington, Vermont 05405

Richard Schattman, Ed.D.
Principal
Swanton Elementary/Central School
24 Fourth Street
Swanton, Vermont 05488

Alice Udvari-Solner, Ph.D.
Assistant Professor
University of Wisconsin–Madison
225 North Mills Street
Room 224A
Madison, Wisconsin 53706

What Are Quick-Guides and How Are They Used?

Many educators whom we meet are anxious to get relevant information on inclusion but find that they don't have enough time to read long articles and books. We have designed the Quick-Guides contained in this book (numbered #6 through #10) to provide helpful advice that can be read in a short amount of time. Guides #6 through #10 expand on information provided in Guides #1 through #5 (***Quick-Guides to Inclusion: Ideas for Educating Students with Disabilities*** [Paul H. Brookes Publishing Co., 1997]).

You may consider each of the Quick-Guides in this book as an individual document that can stand alone, even though the Quick-Guides are interrelated. Each Quick-Guide has

- A letter to the teacher that introduces the content
- A list of 10 Guidelines-at-a-Glance
- A set of the guidelines, each on a separate page, suitable for duplication as overhead transparencies
- A page of text discussing each of the 10 guidelines
- A short list of Selected References

The Quick-Guides are written for general educators, although they can be helpful to a variety of team members. You have permission to photocopy the Quick-Guides from this book to share with your colleagues. We thought this might be especially helpful for those of you who find yourself working with other general educators to facilitate the supported education of students with disabilities. As we shared these Quick-Guides prior to publication, we found they were frequently given to general educators by special education colleagues, were passed out to faculty members by their principals, and were used by staff development specialists and trainers as part of information packets. Some people used them to share information with parents, therapists, community members, school board members, student teachers, and college students.

We encourage you to share them with folks—that's the whole idea! If you have any ideas about future Quick-Guide topics, please feel free to contact me.

Good Luck!
Michael F. Giangreco

Quick-Guides to Inclusion 2

Quick-Guide #6

Adapting the Curriculum

Alice Udvari-Solner

Quick-Guides to Inclusion 2:
Ideas for Educating Students with Disabilities

Michael F. Giangreco, Ph.D.
Series Editor

Quick-Guides to Inclusion 2: Ideas for Educating Students with Disabilities   © 1998 Michael F. Giangreco
Available through Paul H. Brookes Publishing Co., Baltimore: 1-800-638-3775

Dear Teacher,

As educators we are in a profession that allows and often requires us to be creative daily! Just as architects and engineers design structures for living, we design learning environments. Our curricula and instruction are the tools we use to construct these learning places. Through our curriculum decisions and planning, we have the power to create learning environments that are rich, exciting, interactive discovery zones for all students.

As we include students with disabilities in our general education classes, we should reconsider what we have taught in the past and its relevance to our current students and their needs. Teachers who successfully include students with very diverse learning needs recommend taking a multifaceted view of curriculum design. Rather than thinking about the curriculum as a predetermined set of facts and knowledge that the entire class must master, it should be considered a dynamic, ever-changing body of information that provides many learning options for every student. Quite simply, adapting curriculum is creating multiple paths to learning. Teachers do this by rethinking what they will teach or what they have taught in the past and by identifying what is appropriate for specific students to learn.

Adapting the curriculum is just one part of our creative endeavor to help keep our classrooms lively and responsive to the needs of kids. The guidelines that follow outline key points that will help you and other education team members talk about the curriculum and develop multiple learning avenues.

Good Luck!

Alice

1. As a Team, Discuss and Plan Curriculum Together

2. Decide as a Team What "Curriculum" Means

3. Create a Student-Centered Curriculum

4. Get to Know Your Students' Abilities and Interests, and Use Their Expertise

5. Develop a Range of Multilevel Learning Outcomes for Each Student

6. Translate Multilevel Goals into Curriculum

7. Design Learning Experiences to Reflect Multilevel Goals

8. Adapt Instructional Approaches to Promote Active Learning

9. Look for Other Ways to Adapt Your Classroom

10. Don't Stop Now—Do it Again Next Year!

Quick-Guides to Inclusion 2: Ideas for Educating Students with Disabilities   © 1998 Michael F. Giangreco
Available through Paul H. Brookes Publishing Co., Baltimore: 1-800-638-3775

#1

As a Team,
Discuss and Plan
Curriculum Together

Quick-Guides to Inclusion 2: Ideas for Educating Students with Disabilities   © 1998 Michael F. Giangreco
Available through Paul H. Brookes Publishing Co., Baltimore: 1-800-638-3775

In the past teachers were expected and even encouraged to act as the sole decision makers about curricula and instruction for their specific classes. The classroom teacher determined what was important to teach, designed learning activities, developed all the instructional materials, and carried out the instruction—alone. As our classrooms have broadened to include students with more diverse learning needs, it is no longer realistic to expect classroom teachers to teach in isolation. To do our jobs well, communication, cooperation, and collaboration among education team members are essential. This kind of teamwork forms an important building block in creating inclusive classrooms.

Discussions and decisions about what to teach and how to teach are critical components of collaboration between general and special educators. If we intend our classrooms to be truly accommodating to students with diverse needs, then our curricula and instruction must be flexible and open to input and change. Meeting weekly to discuss upcoming curricular activities with colleagues who are involved in the educational programs of your students with disabilities will facilitate common understanding, shared decision making, and joint responsibility for carrying out necessary instructional preparation.

In weekly collaborative team meetings, the general educator can present ideas for upcoming curricular activities or topics to the team for discussion and development. If the unit has been taught in the past, it is important for the team to reflect on how it was structured, what worked, and what didn't work. The team can then further define learning outcomes and activities, keeping particular students in mind who have unique learning needs. During these discussions it is critical that the team consider ideas as "under construction" so that all members can contribute to the development of the curriculum.

Quick-Guides to Inclusion 2: Ideas for Educating Students with Disabilities   © 1998 Michael F. Giangreco
Available through Paul H. Brookes Publishing Co., Baltimore: 1-800-638-3775

#2

Decide as a Team
What "Curriculum" Means

Decide as a Team What "Curriculum" Means

As you begin the year and prepare to include students with disabilities in your classroom, it will be important to have a brief conversation with team members about the meaning or definition of **curriculum.** As you plan together with special educators, parents, and related services providers, a common understanding of the term should help team members be more efficient in their communication with one another and facilitate joint planning of instructional activities and also should help the team determine when adaptation to learning activities is necessary.

Generally, educators can think of curriculum as selected content and planned learning experiences that have educational outcomes. Most teachers see curriculum as much more than just subject matter. Often, teachers want to connect content with important values, concepts, opinions, interactions, and learning strategies that they want their students to acquire.

Some teachers are committed to a multicultural approach to curriculum design. Fostering equity, understanding of cultural diversity, and respect for human differences are guiding elements across all subject areas in this educational approach. Integrated thematic curricula (also referred to as thematic teaching, theme study, and learning across the curriculum) is another common approach. Here, different subject areas (math, reading, social studies) are meaningfully connected to each other in the classroom and the school community using a central theme, issue, or topic as a focus. Some classrooms focus on inquiry-based curriculum that allows teachers and students to investigate selected topics or issues through personal and collective research. Whichever approach is used within a school or a classroom, it should be defined and discussed. Then everyone will be "on the same page" when they discuss the needs of specific students.

Quick-Guides to Inclusion 2: Ideas for Educating Students with Disabilities   © 1998 Michael F. Giangreco
Available through Paul H. Brookes Publishing Co., Baltimore: 1-800-638-3775

#3

Create a Student-Centered Curriculum

Create a Student-Centered Curriculum

If we looked into any American classroom during the first week in September, it would be evident that learning takes place in different ways and at different rates. Each student enters school with a different level of understanding and with unique personal strategies for learning. So it only makes sense that the curriculum should differ for all students. However, when teachers design the curriculum as a rigid set of predefined skills, they often have no choice but to be directed by their preset sequence of skills rather than using what they know about their students to shape the curriculum.

In contrast, a student-centered curriculum reflects who our students are and where they are in the learning process. A student-centered curriculum acknowledges that different elements of learning will be more or less important to different students. This basic sense of individualization is at the heart of an inclusive curriculum. Adaptation to or differentiation in curriculum usually means making variations in the scope, depth, breadth, and complexity of what is taught based on knowledge of the student. The purpose of adapting is to make each learning experience more useful and meaningful.

A common misconception is that when a student with disabilities is included in a general education classroom, the teacher must make exceptional variations in the curriculum. In reality when a student-centered approach is employed, the teacher uses his knowledge of what individual students can do and their unique learning styles to influence the content and complexity of curriculum for any given child. Understanding a student's past learning experiences, prior knowledge, and current interests is the first step in individualizing goals and learning outcomes.

Quick-Guides to Inclusion 2: Ideas for Educating Students with Disabilities   © 1998 Michael F. Giangreco
Available through Paul H. Brookes Publishing Co., Baltimore: 1-800-638-3775

#4

Get to Know
Your Students'
Abilities and Interests,
and Use Their Expertise

Quick-Guides to Inclusion 2: Ideas for Educating Students with Disabilities   © 1998 Michael F. Giangreco
Available through Paul H. Brookes Publishing Co., Baltimore: 1-800-638-3775

Get to Know Your Students' Abilities and Interests, and Use Their Expertise

You can develop and shape curricular themes and units of study by observing in which activities your students choose to participate; which topics elicit excitement; and which issues prompt concern, questions, or inquiry. Discovering students' areas of expertise can be as easy as asking "What are you good at, both in and out of school?" "What have you learned from your family, neighbors, and friends?" or "What have you taught others?" These questions are just as relevant for students with disabilities as they are for other students in the classroom. However, we may need to rely on family members, peers, and past teachers to help identify, elaborate, and share the experiences of students with disabilities.

A ninth-grade English teacher developed an expertise profile of his students based on such questions. He discovered interests, experiences, and abilities among his students that included botany, clothing design, speaking Spanish fluently, cooking and catering, games and storytelling, creative writing, rap music and street rhythm (drumming), drama, and electronic "know-how." This led him to find out that Julie, a student with Down syndrome in his class, had lived in South Africa while in elementary school.

During a unit on folklore, the teacher tapped the experiences of his students by allowing them to select stories from various regions and countries. Julie shared tribal artifacts and literature with the class, including stories from her childhood experiences in South Africa. Based on the class profile, the teacher structured learning opportunities within the context of this curricular unit for students to act out selected folktales in costume, rewrite endings or morals to traditional stories, prepare regional dishes to share during performances, and investigate the origins and evolution of storytelling and musical performance associated with specific folktales.

Quick-Guides to Inclusion 2: Ideas for Educating Students with Disabilities   © 1998 Michael F. Giangreco
Available through Paul H. Brookes Publishing Co., Baltimore: 1-800-638-3775

#5

Develop a Range
of Multilevel Learning
Outcomes for Each Student

Quick-Guides to Inclusion 2: Ideas for Educating Students with Disabilities © 1998 Michael F. Giangreco
Available through Paul H. Brookes Publishing Co., Baltimore: 1-800-638-3775

Develop a Range of Multilevel Learning Outcomes for Each Student

Your first "window" into the learning abilities of a student with disabilities may be reading her individualized education program (IEP). Using this document, you will be able to identify high-priority goals that you can and should infuse into the daily rhythms of the school day. For example, if one of your students has a goal of initiating conversation using her augmentative communication system, you can emphasize this objective at the start of each class, during class discussions, in small-group or cooperative learning sessions, while at lunch, and during any social or free-time activity.

Be aware, however, that your student will be able to learn much more than what is identified in the IEP. Acquiring, extending, refining, and using knowledge meaningfully are all elements of what we want students to know and be able to do. Just as you want to build skills in your students without disabilities, you should also define sensible learning outcomes within each area of curriculum for students with disabilities.

Multilevel goals are individualized learning outcomes that are based on each student's unique needs, skills, interests, and abilities. These student-specific curricular goals can and should affect the scope of the curriculum. You may adjust learning outcomes for a particular student 1) by teaching the same curricular topic but with a more or less complex focus; 2) by addressing the same content but requiring the student to use different response modes to demonstrate his knowledge (e.g., to speak rather than write, to point rather than speak); 3) by increasing or decreasing the rate of completion or the pacing of content; 4) by changing expectations in the level of mastery, degree of quality, or quantity of curricular requirements; or 5) by focusing on similar content that has functional applications.

Quick-Guides to Inclusion 2: Ideas for Educating Students with Disabilities   © 1998 Michael F. Giangreco
Available through Paul H. Brookes Publishing Co., Baltimore: 1-800-638-3775

#6

Translate Multilevel
Goals into Curriculum

A curricular unit under consideration in Ms. Lopez's seventh-grade class was **Learning to Conduct Research.** In the past, Ms. Lopez had focused primarily on the skills that each student needed to write a research report. She had selected the following general learning outcomes for all students: 1) to use note-taking strategies to gather information from written resources, 2) to read for facts and summarize main ideas from reference materials, 3) to paraphrase findings in one's own words, and 4) to use reference skills in the school or local library to select relevant resources.

The class included a student who had multiple disabilities and used nonverbal strategies for communication. Other class members included students with advanced abilities in math and science, students with learning disabilities, and students who spoke English as a second language. The education team selected more challenging learning outcomes for the students with advanced math and science backgrounds. These students' goals were 1) to investigate findings about a recent local or national research project; 2) to gather, analyze, and report quantitative data from the project; 3) to utilize the Internet and call on local experts and researchers for data collection; and 4) to predict, speculate, or theorize about the effects of this research.

For several students with learning disabilities, organizational strategies surfaced as high-priority outcomes. Their goals included sorting and prioritizing information, sequencing content, and validating findings with multiple sources. The student with multiple disabilities needed opportunities to practice and refine communication skills. Therefore, his learning outcomes focused on using his augmentative communication device to conduct interviews as a research-gathering technique and to communicate basic information in a presentation to the class with visual aids and a voice-output device.

Quick-Guides to Inclusion 2: Ideas for Educating Students with Disabilities © 1998 Michael F. Giangreco
Available through Paul H. Brookes Publishing Co., Baltimore: 1-800-638-3775

#7

Design Learning Experiences to Reflect Multilevel Goals

An educator's job is not only to determine the goals behind the curriculum but also to design the learning experiences that lead toward those objectives. Based on the goals selected for students in Ms. Lopez's seventh-grade classroom, the education team decided that students could pursue an individual project or a group investigation. They asked students to select a topic that dealt with environmental protection. Students were allowed to choose their methods of research and presentation and had the option of giving an oral or written report. A group was formed that included the student with multiple disabilities as well as a student labeled as gifted and talented. This student group investigated pollution of a local watershed. They had opportunities to achieve student-specific learning outcomes through interviews with university researchers, communication with environmental protection agencies via the Internet, and the development of a final oral presentation. As the teaching team defined these multilevel outcomes, the curriculum was expanded and fortified. There were now meaningful ways for each learner to be included. The following figure, a planning web, shows how the team differentiated the curriculum so that it reflected the educational goals of the class members.

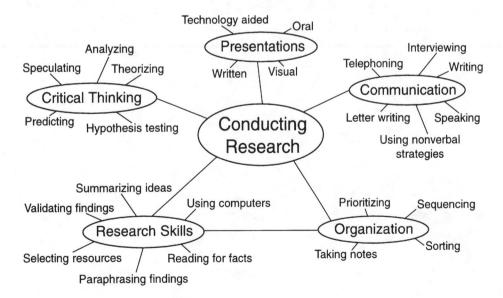

#8

Adapt Instructional Approaches to Promote Active Learning

Quick-Guides to Inclusion 2: Ideas for Educating Students with Disabilities   © 1998 Michael F. Giangreco
Available through Paul H. Brookes Publishing Co., Baltimore: 1-800-638-3775

Adapt Instructional Approaches
to Promote Active Learning

Students with diverse learning needs often have difficulty retaining and applying knowledge when skills are presented to them in isolation or in a passive mode. Active and interactive instructional approaches offer many avenues for involving and engaging students with disabilities. For example, to introduce the unit about conducting research, Ms. Lopez typically provided a lecture outlining the use of resources and the elements of a report. Given the diversity of her students' needs, this instructional approach did not help many of the students in the class to understand the concepts. In collaboration with the special educator, Ms. Lopez adapted her introduction to the unit by handing out newspapers, magazines, telephone books, encyclopedias, videotapes, computer software, names of resource people in the school building, and books.

After arranging for students to work independently, in pairs, or in small groups, she posed this challenge to the class: "Given the resources in front of you, find information for a report on a current environmental issue." As the students explored the resources, Ms. Lopez and the special educator moved around the room to answer questions and observe the students' problem-solving methods. After 30 minutes of exploration, students were asked to share their research strategies, problems, and successes with the class. Using this active learning format, Ms. Lopez engaged all learners, promoted understanding by discovery, and assessed the students' use of resources.

Games, simulations, role plays, interviews, and activity-based and experiential instructional approaches utilize multisensory experiences with real objects, events, processes, and relationships. Teachers can give a context to their curricula by using these active methods.

Quick-Guides to Inclusion 2: Ideas for Educating Students with Disabilities   © 1998 Michael F. Giangreco
Available through Paul H. Brookes Publishing Co., Baltimore: 1-800-638-3775

#9

Look for Other Ways
to Adapt Your Classroom

Look for Other Ways to Adapt Your Classroom

So far we have noted that adapting the curriculum involves redefining relevant learning goals, expanding or shaping content, and designing responsive instructional approaches to reflect curricular decisions. These modifications will be the only accommodations necessary to support the inclusion of some students with disabilities in general education classrooms. However, additional forms of adaptations may be needed to maximize many students' participation and learning.

You may need to make other adaptations to the physical classroom environment, the materials or media used for teaching, student-specific teaching strategies, ancillary support, management techniques, and evaluation strategies. For example, the teacher of the ninth-grade English class studying folklore used other types of adaptations. In order for Julie, the young woman with Down syndrome, to learn her lines as narrator for the folktale performance, she needed a written script that used simplified language. Each page of the script had only two lines of large type; these were in bold print so that visual distractions were reduced. To help Julie learn her lines, a classmate recorded the script on audiotape with appropriate pauses so that Julie could recite the lines after hearing the model.

During skit practices the speech-language pathologist joined the class and worked with Julie's group to facilitate techniques to increase her speech fluency, rate, and articulation. During the actual performance, Julie had a difficult time reciting her lines accurately while still keeping track of the sequence of the skit. A classmate provided support by gently tapping her arm as a physical cue to begin or to stop the narration at appropriate times. Julie's grade for the unit was based on meeting her language and communication goals, cooperating within the group, and producing a one-page summary of the origin of the folktale.

Quick-Guides to Inclusion 2: Ideas for Educating Students with Disabilities © 1998 Michael F. Giangreco
Available through Paul H. Brookes Publishing Co., Baltimore: 1-800-638-3775

#10

Don't Stop Now—
Do it Again Next Year!

Don't Stop Now—Do it Again Next Year!

Thinking about curriculum in a flexible, multilevel manner helps us to revive and rejuvenate our current teaching practices. This is not something we do once and stop. If at the beginning of the year you catch yourself saying "This is the way I've always taught the unit on wolves," stop, and ask yourself a few important questions: "Is the scope and complexity of the curriculum appropriate for all the learners in my classroom this year?" "What do I know or need to know about my students' abilities and expertise that will help me make decisions about the curriculum?" "Do I need to devise specific goals to make the curriculum accessible and more meaningful for specific students?" The answers to these questions will depend on the unique makeup of your class membership, which will change every year.

Each year you will need to renew old relationships and forge new collaborative relationships with special educators, support staff, and parents. Therefore, education teams will revisit and revise curricular decisions if necessary. Teachers have found that with each new year, communication with colleagues becomes more efficient and ideas are developed more readily based on the successful endeavors of previous years. Use simple, agreed-on strategies to adapt your curriculum; this will help make your general education classroom an environment in which all students, including those with disabilities, can thrive.

Quick-Guides to Inclusion 2: Ideas for Educating Students with Disabilities © 1998 Michael F. Giangreco
Available through Paul H. Brookes Publishing Co., Baltimore: 1-800-638-3775

Selected References

Beane, J. (1995). *Toward a coherent curriculum: 1995 yearbook of the Association for Supervision and Curriculum Development*. Alexandria, VA: Association for Supervision and Curriculum Development.

Grennon-Brooks, J., & Brooks, M. (1993). *A case for a constructivist classroom*. Alexandria, VA: Association for Supervision and Curriculum Development.

Heron, E., & Jorgensen, C. (December 1994/January 1995) Addressing learning differences right from the start. *Educational Leadership, 52*(4), 56–58.

Seely, A. (1995). *Integrated thematic units*. Westminster, CA: Teacher Created Materials.

Stainback, S., & Stainback, W. (1992). *Curriculum considerations in inclusive classrooms: Facilitating learning for all students*. Baltimore: Paul H. Brookes Publishing Co.

Udvari-Solner, A. (1996). Accommodating approaches for diverse learners in inclusive classrooms. In L. Power-deFur & F. Orelove (Eds.), *Inclusive education: Practical implementation of the least restrictive environment* (pp. 75–90). Rockville, MD: Aspen Publishers.

Udvari-Solner, A. (1996). Examining teacher thinking: Constructing a process to design curricular adaptations. *Remedial and Special Education, 17*(4), 245–254.

Udvari-Solner, A., & Thousand, J. (1996). Creating a responsive curriculum for inclusive schools. *Remedial and Special Education, 17*(3), 182–192.

Instructional Strategies

Michael F. Giangreco and Lia Cravedi-Cheng

Quick-Guides to Inclusion 2:
Ideas for Educating Students with Disabilities

Michael F. Giangreco, Ph.D.
Series Editor

Quick-Guides to Inclusion 2: Ideas for Educating Students with Disabilities © 1998 Michael F. Giangreco
Available through Paul H. Brookes Publishing Co., Baltimore: 1-800-638-3775

Dear Team Member,

Everybody is concerned about the quality of instruction offered by our schools because, in one way or another, it affects everyone in our community. The reflection, problem solving, and action required to address a specific student's learning needs help us gain new insights and skills we can apply to help other students learn.

Many general and special educators used to assume that general education teachers could not successfully teach students with disabilities, so those students were sent to special education classes. In far too many cases, they encountered low expectations and had limited access to peers without disabilities, too much instructional "downtime," and questionable curriculum. In a small number of situations, students did receive better instruction that was data-based, replicable, and guided by sound principles of learning, which was sometimes referred to as "systematic instruction." Although more systematic instruction may have been technically stellar, too frequently it 1) was applied to questionable curriculum content; 2) was applied out of context; 3) limited students' access to typical places, activities, and relationships; and 4) ignored students' learning styles. Placing students in inclusive classes sets the stage to address these problems, but it is not enough. Many people have suggested using systematic instruction in general education classrooms, but it hasn't fit as well as it has when used in special education classes. Our challenge is to apply these time-tested ideas about good teaching in new and contextually viable ways. These are instructional strategies you already know. Remember, the principles of teaching and learning don't change just because someone puts a label on a child; these methods just need some adaptation so you can meet the unique needs of the child.

Good Luck!

Michael and Lia

1. Know Each Student's Characteristics and Learning Styles

2. Choose Meaningful Learning Outcomes

3. Establish Shared Expectations

4. Use Good Teaching Methods

5. Use More Good Teaching Methods

6. Use Even More Good Teaching Methods

7. Plan How to Address Learning Outcomes in Classroom Activities

8. Provide Sufficient Learning Opportunities, and Be Consistent

9. Collect Data on Student Learning

10. Use Data to Make Instructional Decisions

Quick-Guides to Inclusion 2: Ideas for Educating Students with Disabilities © 1998 Michael F. Giangreco
Available through Paul H. Brookes Publishing Co., Baltimore: 1-800-638-3775

#1

Know
Each Student's
Characteristics
and Learning Styles

Know Each Student's Characteristics and Learning Styles

It may seem almost too obvious to mention, but good instruction begins by knowing the student's characteristics and learning styles across a variety of dimensions. Often education teams unproductively focus too much on a student's disabilities or perceived impairments. Although those characteristics may be too important to ignore, it is more helpful to consider students' attributes and abilities when you design instruction and select environments conducive to learning. For example, knowing that a student is blind eliminates certain visual approaches to instruction but doesn't provide constructive information on which to build. Conversely, knowing that a student who is blind has good tactile discrimination abilities is much more useful from an instructional standpoint.

You may draw information about students' characteristics and abilities from many potential sources such as parent interviews, reports from support service specialists, direct observations, and conversations with last year's teacher—but nothing can replace the knowledge you will gain through ongoing, personal teaching interactions with students.

Ask yourself what you know about each student's abilities and characteristics in these categories:

1. **Cognitive** (e.g., has good categorization and memory skills)
2. **Physical** (e.g., has consistent motor control over head movements side to side, has functional use of right hand)
3. **Sensory** (e.g., can orient toward the source of sounds, prefers using materials with smooth textures)
4. **Social/Emotional** (e.g., has an even temperament, is very sociable, enjoys interactions with peers)
5. **Motivational** (e.g., is motivated by participation in games and activities)
6. **Interactional** (e.g., prefers working in small groups)
7. **Creative** (e.g., likes drawing and performing in plays, likes folk music)

Use these categories to design instruction that builds on each student's strengths and preferences.

Quick-Guides to Inclusion 2: Ideas for Educating Students with Disabilities   © 1998 Michael F. Giangreco
Available through Paul H. Brookes Publishing Co., Baltimore: 1-800-638-3775

#2

Choose Meaningful
Learning Outcomes

Even the best instructional strategies are of limited value unless they are applied to helping students learn something important. Therefore, selecting meaningful learning outcomes is an essential precondition of quality instruction. So what are important learning outcomes? State and local school officials are addressing this ever-evolving question more frequently than ever before. Working with community members, they are establishing educational standards designed to reflect learning outcomes that are considered important for all children. People here in our home state, Vermont, have been developing local standards based on *Vermont's Common Core Framework for Curriculum and Assessment* (Vermont Department of Education, 1996). The **Common Core** consists of two main categories of standards: 1) **Vital Results** (i.e., communication, reasoning and problem solving, personal development, and civic/social responsibility) and 2) **Fields of Knowledge** (i.e., arts, language, and literature; history and social sciences; and science, mathematics, and technology). Local schools in Vermont use this framework to develop curricula that address local and state standards.

Although standards are helpful in ensuring that all students, including those with disabilities, receive a well-rounded education, one of the hallmarks of special education is providing *individualized* education. Sometimes appropriate individualization requires selecting learning outcomes that extend beyond the boundaries of the traditional curriculum. When selecting individually important learning outcomes, you should consider criteria such as 1) functionality, 2) frequency of use, 3) age appropriateness, 4) ongoing and future usefulness, 5) student preference, 6) parental priority, and 7) immediacy of need. Our time to work with students is limited, so it is critical that we teach learning outcomes that are important to each student and valued in the greater community.

Quick-Guides to Inclusion 2: Ideas for Educating Students with Disabilities © 1998 Michael F. Giangreco
Available through Paul H. Brookes Publishing Co., Baltimore: 1-800-638-3775

#3

Establish
Shared Expectations

Establish Shared Expectations

A common source of anxiety for classroom teachers is understanding what others, such as parents, administrators, and special educators, expect of them. Classroom teachers frequently ask "Do you expect me to teach students with disabilities most or all of what I teach the other students without disabilities?" Whether administrators, special educators, and parents answer "yes" or "no," it is important to ensure that everyone shares a common expectation of what students with disabilities should learn and who will be responsible for which part of the teaching process. Certainly the adults involved in teaching the children need to talk about this, but far too often students are left out of this loop inappropriately. To provide good instruction, educators must choose challenging but reasonably attainable goals for their students and make students aware of these expectations. Students should receive an ever-increasing voice in designing their own learning activities. Self-advocating and making choices of this sort are critical aspects of personal development.

You and the rest of the team should start by identifying a small, individualized set of learning priorities—often ones that are rooted in student- and family-centered perspectives. Next, agree on a larger set of additional learning outcomes that make up an overall educational program based on local or state standards. These learning outcomes may include goals that extend beyond what is typically part of the general curriculum. Many students with disabilities also need to receive general supports and services that allow for their participation in class.

It may be helpful if you use a one- to two-page Program-at-a-Glance to summarize the student's educational program in three parts: 1) priorities, 2) other learning outcomes, and 3) general supports. Clarifying expectations by using this type of concise listing can assist you in planning and scheduling; serve as a helpful reminder of the student's individualized needs; and provide an effective way to communicate the student's needs to special subject teachers such as art, music, and physical education teachers.

Quick-Guides to Inclusion 2: Ideas for Educating Students with Disabilities   © 1998 Michael F. Giangreco
Available through Paul H. Brookes Publishing Co., Baltimore: 1-800-638-3775

#4

Use Good
Teaching Methods

Use Good Teaching Methods

The vast majority of students with disabilities respond favorably to many of the same teaching methods that are effective with students who do not have disabilities. These common methods include modeling and demonstrating, holding class discussions, practicing, guiding discovery, conducting experiments, taking field trips, offering participatory activities, using multimedia technology, employing question-asking strategies, handling manipulative materials, using educational games and play, demonstrating positive and negative examples, giving corrective feedback, and assigning individual or small-group projects.

Challenges arise when students do not progress adequately when you have used typical instructional methods. In such cases, you must augment instruction with more precisely applied methods. Guidelines #5 and #6 contain instructional methods that you can apply within the context of typical class activities. Don't be intimidated by the technical names that come from the field of applied behavior analysis (Alberto & Troutman, 1995; Snell & Brown, 1993) because you will recognize that you have used many or all of these strategies before. Choose from these methods based on 1) which method or combination of methods is most likely to be effective based on your knowledge of the student's characteristics, 2) which learning outcomes you have identified, and 3) which method you can apply in the most status-neutral or status-enhancing way in typical settings.

If you've ever taught a child to tie shoelaces or do long division, you may have used **task analysis.** Task analysis involves breaking a skill down into its component parts to help students learn the skill. Sometimes these components are fairly large chunks of behavior; at other times they are very small. Each step in a task analysis has a built-in prompt for the next step. If you find that a student has a problem with only one particular part of a skill, then that may be the only part that you need to teach through task analysis. (See Guidelines #5 and #6 for more methods.)

Quick-Guides to Inclusion 2: Ideas for Educating Students with Disabilities   © 1998 Michael F. Giangreco
Available through Paul H. Brookes Publishing Co., Baltimore: 1-800-638-3775

#5

Use More
Good Teaching Methods

If you've ever taught a child how to dress himself, you've probably used some form of **chaining,** such as **continuous chaining** (all steps of the task analysis are taught), **forward chaining** (steps are taught from the beginning of the sequence until the student makes an error; instruction proceeds only after the step is mastered), and **backward chaining** (the last step only is taught until it is mastered; the teacher then moves backward through the sequence, adding one step at a time until reaching the beginning). When using backward chaining to teach a child to zip her coat, you would complete all the steps except pulling the zipper the last few inches. Ask her to pull the zipper the last few inches, then ask her to pull the zipper from near the bottom, then ask her to join the two parts of the zipper together and to zip the coat by herself.

If you've ever taught a child how to ride a bike, cross the street, or dial a telephone, you may have used **errorless learning.** Errorless learning refers to guiding a student through a task by using sufficient prompts so that the student successfully finishes the task as quickly as possible while making as few errors as possible. The teacher interrupts errors as they occur and provides guidance. As the student becomes more proficient, guidance is faded. Errorless learning provides repeated opportunities for practicing a skill correctly and is useful for tasks in which errors could be dangerous (e.g., crossing the street).

If you've ever taught a child how to read a clock face, you may have used **cue redundancy.** Cue redundancy involves exaggerating the relevant dimension of a cue to help the child discriminate between it and other cues. For example, when teaching the difference between a clock's hour and minute hands by using cue redundancy, length (not color or shape) is the relevant dimension that you would exaggerate by making the hour hand very short and the minute hand very long. You would gradually change the hands to more typical lengths. (See Guideline #6 for more methods.)

Quick-Guides to Inclusion 2: Ideas for Educating Students with Disabilities   © 1998 Michael F. Giangreco
Available through Paul H. Brookes Publishing Co., Baltimore: 1-800-638-3775

#6

Use Even More
Good Teaching Methods

If you've ever taught a child how to compose a story, you've probably used **shaping**. When you use shaping, you simply reinforce increasingly proficient approximations of the target skill. For example, teachers expect increasing detail, description, spelling accuracy, and proper use of grammar in students' compositions. Shaping is a developmental process of starting at the student's current level and moving forward at her own pace.

If you've ever taught a child early handwriting skills, you've probably given **prompts** and **cues.** Prompts and cues include full physical guidance, partial physical guidance, modeling, verbal directions, questions, reminders, encouragement, and visual clues. You can provide prompts and cues prior to or following student responses and should fade prompts and cues as quickly as possible. For example, using dotted lines and letter shapes in handwriting instruction is a cue that you can fade.

If you've ever taught a child to say "thank you" in response to receiving something, you've probably used **time delay.** Time delay refers to the pairing of two cues simultaneously (zero delay), one cue to which you know the student will respond correctly and another cue (often natural) to which you would like the student to respond. For example, when teaching a young child to say "thank you," you want him to respond to the natural cue of receiving an object. You can start teaching this by simultaneously pairing the natural cue (receiving something) with the extra cue: "Say 'thank you.'" When he repeats "thank you," you can insert a time delay (e.g., a couple of seconds) between the natural cue and the extra cue and gradually increase the delay. When the time delay is long enough, he will respond with "thank you" before receiving the extra cue. Fade extra cues at the same time that you increase the time delay (e.g., replace "Say 'thank you'" or "What do you say?" with an expectant look). Time delay can be especially helpful for teaching students who are not imitative.

Quick-Guides to Inclusion 2: Ideas for Educating Students with Disabilities   © 1998 Michael F. Giangreco
Available through Paul H. Brookes Publishing Co., Baltimore: 1-800-638-3775

#7

Plan How to Address
Learning Outcomes
in Classroom Activities

Plan How to Address Learning Outcomes in Classroom Activities

Planning an inclusive lesson requires the teacher to piece together creatively many bits of knowledge. This begins by identifying individual learning outcomes for each student in the group, whether the group is large or small. Although students with disabilities may have the same learning outcomes as their peers without disabilities during some activities, frequently their learning outcomes are different. They may be slightly or significantly different in scope or in content within the same curriculum area (e.g., social studies). At other times a student's learning outcomes may come from a different curriculum area than the activity that they are completing. For example, a student may be participating in a science experiment but focusing on communication and literacy outcomes such as "describes an observation verbally and in writing." When it's not obvious, you can use variations of the Osborn-Parnes Creative Problem-Solving Process (Giangreco, Cloninger, Dennis, & Edelman, 1994; Parnes, 1981) to figure out which individualized learning outcomes are suited to particular class activities.

Once you have identified the class activity and learning outcomes, you should ask a series of basic questions to plan the lesson. First, ask "What will I do as a teacher?" Your answer should include factors such as environmental arrangements, student groupings, materials used, directions given, and extra cues provided. Second, ask "What does it look like when the student responds correctly?" You should look for observable behavior(s) rather than a single type of correct response. Third, ask "What will you do if the student responds correctly, does not respond, or responds incorrectly?" You must be prepared for these possibilities and may need to include in your lesson such components as feedback, reinforcement, correction procedures, prompts, more time for responding, or additional opportunities for responding. Fourth, ask "How will you describe, measure, and document student progress so that it can be used to facilitate learning?" Remember, instruction is a cyclical, continuing process.

Quick-Guides to Inclusion 2: Ideas for Educating Students with Disabilities   © 1998 Michael F. Giangreco
Available through Paul H. Brookes Publishing Co., Baltimore: 1-800-638-3775

#8

Provide Sufficient Learning Opportunities, and Be Consistent

Provide Sufficient Learning Opportunities, and Be Consistent

Most students require frequent opportunities to interact with content or to practice a skill in order to learn it. In fact, sometimes students with disabilities need even more opportunities than their peers without disabilities. As you think about how to address learning outcomes in classroom activities, you should also think about the various opportunities you can provide for students to experience those outcomes. For example, if a student has the learning outcome "initiates interactions with peers," it would be important for you to consider appropriate times when the student could practice that skill within an activity or series of activities planned for the day or the week. If students work in pairs or in small groups, they will have appropriate and naturally occurring opportunities. You can use an activity/goal matrix to help identify learning opportunities (Giangreco, Cloninger, & Iverson, 1998). Remember, it is also okay to ask for help. There are people in your school or community who can help you identify opportunities for students to practice target skills.

Just as students need multiple opportunities to interact with content and need to practice skills at different times and in different situations, students also need to experience consistency. If you have decided to cue or to reinforce a skill in certain ways, you and other classroom staff (and maybe even students) need to feel comfortable enough with those procedures to use them consistently. To be truthful, this is sometimes difficult; you may make mistakes, but that's unavoidable. What matters is that you are thinking consciously about your teaching methods and are doing your best to be consistent. As you consider how to provide consistent learning experiences, think beyond the immediate classroom staff to special area teachers, office staff, cafeteria staff, and schoolmates. Pursue this extent of consistency only in situations in which it is critical. Some naturally occurring variation in learning experience and reinforcement can facilitate generalization across settings, people, and cues, which is desirable for optimal achievement.

Quick-Guides to Inclusion 2: Ideas for Educating Students with Disabilities   © 1998 Michael F. Giangreco
Available through Paul H. Brookes Publishing Co., Baltimore: 1-800-638-3775

#9

Collect Data
on Student Learning

Collect Data on Student Learning

Teachers often have an intuitive sense of how their students are progressing. In order to validate those impressions, it is important to gather additional information through some form(s) of systematic data collection. Encourage your colleagues to value data collection because it provides an index of professional accountability and serves as a vital step in the teaching/learning cycle.

To measure progress, you must first focus on the learning outcomes you have identified for the student and translate them into behaviors that you can observe and document. You then need to select a method for evaluating the behaviors. There are many ways to do this, and you probably already use a number of them. Quizzes, tests, projects, observations, demonstrations, and work samples are all useful measures of progress. These various indicators can tell you information such as 1) the percentage of accuracy the student has achieved, 2) the frequency with which the student uses a skill, 3) the rate at which the student accomplishes a task, 4) the quality of work the student generates, 5) the length of time a student's attention can be sustained, 6) the number of steps in a series (i.e., from a task analysis) the student can successfully complete, and 7) the way that the student's quality of life has improved as a result of working toward certain learning outcomes.

The data collection methods you choose and the information for which you look should be directly related to the student's learning outcomes. For example, think back to the learning outcome mentioned in Guideline #8: "initiates interactions with peers." Given that stated outcome, you might want to observe the student to measure the frequency of interactions with classmates during small working groups. A student's team should agree on data collection methods, and a variety of team members, including the student, should collect data.

Quick-Guides to Inclusion 2: Ideas for Educating Students with Disabilities © 1998 Michael F. Giangreco
Available through Paul H. Brookes Publishing Co., Baltimore: 1-800-638-3775

#10

Use Data to Make
Instructional Decisions

Now you have some ideas about how to collect data about students' progress toward their learning outcomes. What's next?! You can use the data that you collect in an active way—to lead you to understand the students' current and future instructional needs.

In order to do this, you first need to think about 1) the level at which the student is currently performing, 2) the level at which the student needs to perform in order to achieve an educational outcome, 3) how much time it might take for the student to meet this goal, 4) how frequently you will collect information about the student's progress, and 5) when you should review the data to see if the student has reached the goal. If you merely collect data—without reviewing and using it—you may as well not collect the data at all.

Once you have some data about student progress to look at, you need to ask yourself what the information tells you. It may show that the student 1) is ready to move to a new outcome or a higher level of performance with that outcome, 2) needs more time to accomplish the outcome, or 3) requires more or different teaching strategies.

After the team has assessed a student's progress, it is time to consider possible actions, select a course of action, and take that action. Although it is common and appropriate to consider instructional and curricular changes, in some cases you may also need to change your data collection methods. Your existing methods may not provide you with the information you are seeking or may not be sensitive enough to detect moderate levels of progress. The data that you collect will inform the decisions you make about your assessment process and instructional program.

Quick-Guides to Inclusion 2: Ideas for Educating Students with Disabilities   © 1998 Michael F. Giangreco
Available through Paul H. Brookes Publishing Co., Baltimore: 1-800-638-3775

Selected References

Alberto, P.A., & Troutman, A.C. (1995). *Applied behavior analysis for teachers* (4th ed.). Upper Saddle River, NJ: Prentice-Hall.

Armstrong, T. (1994). *Multiple intelligences in the classroom.* Alexandria, VA: Association for Supervision and Curriculum Development.

Gardner, H. (1983). *Frames of mind: The theory of multiple intelligences.* New York: HarperCollins.

Giangreco, M.F., Cloninger, C.J., Dennis, R.E., & Edelman, S.W. (1994). Problem-solving methods to facilitate inclusive education. In J.S. Thousand, R.A. Villa, & A.I. Nevin (Eds.), *Creativity and collaborative learning: A practical guide to empowering students and teachers* (pp. 321–346). Baltimore: Paul H. Brookes Publishing Co.

Giangreco, M.F., Cloninger, C.J., & Iverson, V.S. (1998). *Choosing outcomes and accommodations for children (COACH): A guide to educational planning for students with disabilities* (2nd ed.). Baltimore: Paul H. Brookes Publishing Co.

Parnes, S.J. (1981). *The magic of your mind.* Buffalo, NY: Creative Education Foundation in association with Bearly Ltd.

Snell, M.E., & Brown, F. (1993). Instructional planning and implementation. In M.E. Snell (Ed.), *Instruction of students with severe disabilities* (4th ed.). New York: Merrill Education.

Vermont Department of Education. (1996). *Vermont's Common Core framework for curriculum and assessment.* Montpelier: Author.

Quick-Guide #8

Communication Systems
in the Classroom

Janet M. Duncan and Patricia A. Prelock

Quick-Guides to Inclusion 2:
Ideas for Educating Students with Disabilities

Michael F. Giangreco, Ph.D.
Series Editor

Quick-Guides to Inclusion 2: Ideas for Educating Students with Disabilities   © 1998 Michael F. Giangreco
Available through Paul H. Brookes Publishing Co., Baltimore: 1-800-638-3775

Dear Teacher,

Sometimes people make incorrect assumptions about a person with a disability because he does not speak in a typical way. Just because someone does not speak does not mean that he does not understand or that he has nothing to say. Some students with disabilities require specialized systems or devices to communicate. These ways of communicating are called **augmentative and alternative communication, or AAC.**

AAC includes pointing, gesturing, and eye gazing, as well as using sign language, letterboards, picture symbols, drawings, photographs, keyboards, computer-generated speech, and other forms of computer assistance. Some students use AAC to augment their speech, whereas others use it as an alternative to speech. Some students use more than one type of augmentative system or a combination of systems, depending on the situation and their communication partner.

Whatever system a student uses, it is important for you to become comfortable with it and to know how to communicate with the student. This will require getting to know the student and the unique aspects of the student's communication system. These guidelines will help you think about strategies for including students who use AAC in class routines so that they always have opportunities for communication, both receptively and expressively. As you become more knowledgeable about your students' communication, you can share what you have learned with your other students so they can become skillful communication partners in both academic and social situations. It is important to remember that using AAC is simply another way for a student to communicate.

Good Luck!

Janet and Patty

GUIDELINES-AT-A-GLANCE

1. Learn About Each Student's Preferred Communication

2. Provide Each Student with the Necessary Supports to Communicate

3. Create a Communication-Friendly Environment

4. Make Sure Each Student Has a Way to Communicate at All Times

5. Involve Classmates as Communication Partners

6. Honor Your Student's Communication

7. Use Natural Experiences and Direct Teaching to Foster Communication

8. Avoid Becoming Overly Dependent on High-Technology Devices

9. Update Communication Systems Frequently

10. Evaluate Communication Progress

Quick-Guides to Inclusion 2: Ideas for Educating Students with Disabilities   © 1998 Michael F. Giangreco
Available through Paul H. Brookes Publishing Co., Baltimore: 1-800-638-3775

#1

Learn About
Each Student's
Preferred Communication

Learn About Each
Student's Preferred Communication

Verbal communication is not the only way that individuals let us know what they want to say. All behavior, including body language, communicates messages. Most typical speakers use these modes of communication to enhance their verbal messages. A student who does not use speech as her primary means of communication may point, look, gesture, sign, or use a variety of symbols (e.g., objects, pictures, printed words) to convey her message. It is important to learn your student's communicative strengths and preferences because communication systems selected for individual students should capitalize on strengths and increase potential for becoming independent communicators.

When selecting a student's communication system, the first step is to identify his level of communicative intent. You need to know that if he attempts to communicate, the resulting message is what he desired or intended to convey. The student's level of understanding is another critical factor during the selection of both expressive and receptive modes of communication. (In addition, you should always be attuned to changes in the student's comprehension.)

When selecting a communication system, you and the other team members should look for a device that is portable and that has symbols with a high degree of **iconicity.** Iconicity refers to how much a symbol looks like what it represents (Lloyd & Blischak, 1992, p. 106); a highly iconic symbol resembles its referent closely. Portability and iconicity will allow the student to participate, with little delay, in communicative interactions. The communication system should also be accessible to a variety of communication partners, including both peers and adults.

Once a communication system is selected, it requires timely programming so that vocabulary can be expanded and/or curricular themes can be incorporated. Effective implementation of any communication system requires the thoughtful reflection of a team of individuals, including the child and his parents, the general classroom teacher, special educators, and AAC specialists. As a team member, make sure you know the basics about your student's communication so that you can select and implement the most effective AAC system.

Quick-Guides to Inclusion 2: Ideas for Educating Students with Disabilities   © 1998 Michael F. Giangreco
Available through Paul H. Brookes Publishing Co., Baltimore: 1-800-638-3775

#2

Provide Each Student with the Necessary Supports to Communicate

---

Provide Each Student with the Necessary Supports to Communicate

To effectively use a communication system, a student who uses AAC may need various forms of assistance, such as physical or sensory support, another person's guidance, or attitudinal support. Your student may need any or all of these supports depending on his individual needs and the situation.

Physical or sensory support is particularly important for a student who has coordination, mobility, hearing, or vision impairments. Your first step should be to make sure your student is comfortably positioned in a way that allows her to communicate. Sometimes parents or special education staff can recommend warm-up exercises to improve mobility or tips to maximize sensory capabilities.

A variety of AAC team members (e.g., physical and occupational therapists, speech-language pathologists, special educators, vision and hearing specialists) may be especially helpful in determining appropriate physical or sensory supports or equipment. They may notice small but important environmental factors that can make a difference in a student's ability to communicate (e.g., seat height, lighting, background noise, position of materials, tactile characteristics).

A classmate or adult may have to help the student use his communication system. For example, the student may need help to turn on a computer or to access the software. She may need a communication partner who knows the communication system (e.g., American Sign Language). Other students may need physical prompts, assistance, or guidance when communicating.

Physical and sensory supports are best enhanced by an atmosphere of attitudinal support whereby the students' communication partners constantly encourage and respect communication and approach the person as a competent communicator. Such attitudinal support is necessary even in situations in which it is unclear whether the student understands the entire exchange; this is the "least dangerous assumption" that you and other communication partners can make (Donnellan, 1984, p. 141).

#3

Create a
Communication-Friendly
Environment

Create a Communication-Friendly Environment

Developing an awareness among other students and school personnel of the AAC system used by your student is the first step you can take to create a communication-friendly environment. In other words, helping all of your students and school staff achieve a level of familiarity with the AAC system makes its use become ordinary and typical.

In classrooms that are naturally language-rich environments (e.g., classrooms that have language experience charts, interactive bulletin boards, predictable stories, or big books), AAC system use should be built in to all those naturally occurring opportunities to use language. Students who use AAC systems will benefit from exposure to print and spoken language, whereas students without disabilities will learn valuable communication and social skills by interacting with a classmate using AAC (e.g., active listening, turn taking). Teachers can model these skills for students through their daily interactions.

Teachers can show all students alternative ways to communicate, including but not limited to use of the student's AAC system. You might ask students "How can you communicate your ideas other than by speaking or by writing?" All students can be encouraged to use aids such as computer graphics, gestures, or dramatic presentation to augment their spoken and written communication. Such approaches can help you identify each of your students' preferred learning styles. You can also teach your students sign language or other ways to communicate.

By modeling the value and use of a student's AAC system, you can set a powerful example for your students. As students develop an understanding of the AAC system, their sense of community with one another will grow along with their acceptance of the student who uses the system.

Quick-Guides to Inclusion 2: Ideas for Educating Students with Disabilities   © 1998 Michael F. Giangreco
Available through Paul H. Brookes Publishing Co., Baltimore: 1-800-638-3775

#4

Make Sure Each Student Has a Way to Communicate at All Times

Make Sure Each Student Has a Way to Communicate at All Times

Imagine how frustrating it would be if you were not able to communicate, even for a brief period of time. This is why it is imperative that students who rely on AAC systems to communicate have access to their own system or a back-up system at all times.

Although speech, gestures, and sign language are examples of communication systems that do not require special equipment, some students who use AAC do need devices to communicate. Sometimes this equipment can be as small and technologically basic as a **communication wallet** with photographs or drawings. At other times it can be as sophisticated and technologically advanced as an individualized computer system. Portability is always a concern when selecting a communication system because a highly portable system allows the student to have access to a means of communication at all times. The less portable the system, the greater the likelihood that it will be left behind, for example, when the student leaves the classroom to go to the cafeteria, to the playground, to the gymnasium, or on field trips.

Even when a student effectively uses a communication device, it is crucial to develop back-up systems for times when the device is forgotten, misplaced, or broken. To prevent gaps in communication, it is valuable to encourage the student to use multiple communication methods. For example, a student who uses a voice-output keyboard may opt to carry a small laminated letterboard in a pocket folder. Other back-up systems may involve hand signs, vocalizations, picture symbols, gestures, or eye movements. Using multiple ways to communicate encourages the student to use speech when he can or in situations in which it is appropriate. For example, a student may first try to communicate by using speech. If his communication partner does not understand him, he can use augmentative or alternative approaches to make his meaning more clear (e.g., pointing to an object or picture, miming an action, drawing a picture).

Quick-Guides to Inclusion 2: Ideas for Educating Students with Disabilities   © 1998 Michael F. Giangreco
Available through Paul H. Brookes Publishing Co., Baltimore: 1-800-638-3775

#5

Involve Classmates
as Communication Partners

Involve Classmates as Communication Partners

If a student is to communicate successfully using an AAC system, it is imperative for her to have as many communication partners as possible. Classmates are invaluable as willing communication partners. Sometimes, when a student is learning to use an AAC system, teachers tend to think of the process as something very specialized to be addressed only by a speech-language pathologist or special educator. This need not be the case. Students want and need to communicate with other students, and these interactions are essential for developing social relationships and for enhancing self-image. By communicating with one another, students learn so much from each other.

You can support students who use AAC by helping their classmates learn the communication system. You can share information about the AAC system early in the school year. A detailed explanation of AAC is not necessary; rather, explain to the students how the individual communicates best. The student who uses AAC and his parents can help by demonstrating for classmates how the AAC system works. Throughout this process, it is important to maintain the student's dignity and respectfully handle his AAC system.

Students may choose one or two classmates to whom they will teach their system first and expand from there. You can help by modeling effective communication interactions on several occasions and by providing opportunities for communication before assuming the students are capable partners for the individual who uses AAC. At the same time, give students the privacy and space to interact without always being "shadowed" by adults. Peers often become advocates for each other, and this is especially important for students who use AAC. You may find that peers are just as knowledgeable as the school staff about the student and her AAC system.

Quick-Guides to Inclusion 2: Ideas for Educating Students with Disabilities   © 1998 Michael F. Giangreco
Available through Paul H. Brookes Publishing Co., Baltimore: 1-800-638-3775

#6

Honor Your
Student's Communication

Honor Your Student's Communication

Regardless of how simple or sophisticated the AAC system is, it is important to honor the communication expressed by the student who uses the system. At its most basic level, this means responding to his communication. For example, if the student requests a drink by pointing to a cup on his communication board, the strongest response would be to provide a drink immediately. At the early stages of learning, you want the student to understand that using the AAC system is a powerful tool for affecting his personal world. You may not always like or agree with what a student has to say. It is crucial, however, for the student to know that you hear and respect his communication.

Sometimes circumstances will not permit you to address every request in such an immediate manner. In these cases, you should acknowledge the student's request and address it as soon as possible, at which time you should use the AAC system again to teach the connection between system use and the response to the request.

Honoring a student's communication also requires you to make sure that she has communication partners. Sometimes students who have communication boards on their lap trays make silent selections that no one notices, and their communication is not acknowledged. If people are not always present to notice these types of expressions, the student may need a signaling device to get the attention of a communication partner.

Finally, it is important for you to provide privacy for communication because many forms of AAC are highly visible and can be seen and understood by others without the AAC user's approval or knowledge. It is also important for communication partners to assist the student in selecting privacy if needed, for example, by being aware of the orientation of the communication display in relation to other people. You should also allow privacy for written communication, such as by deleting messages from computer screens, shredding printouts, or putting printed communication in a folder marked **confidential.**

Quick-Guides to Inclusion 2: Ideas for Educating Students with Disabilities   © 1998 Michael F. Giangreco
Available through Paul H. Brookes Publishing Co., Baltimore: 1-800-638-3775

#7

Use Natural Experiences and Direct Teaching to Foster Communication

---

Use Natural Experiences and Direct Teaching to Foster Communication

To learn to use a communication system effectively, students and their communication partners need naturally occurring opportunities to communicate and also require direct teaching and practice. An AAC specialist can help the team identify these natural opportunities as well as provide support regarding direct instructional approaches. For example, some students will need extra cues or prompts, help responding to natural cues, or intensive practice. This doesn't necessarily mean that a specialist will always deliver the instruction. A specialist's help, however, is appropriate at certain times because merely providing a student with an AAC device or system is not enough. The team will decide which approach works best for each student and who should provide instruction for various parts of the learning process.

Students need instruction to learn the system and real opportunities to use their communication skills. This instruction and application can occur concurrently. Too often students are required to learn skills in isolation before they can apply these skills in more natural contexts. Learning in isolation is undesirable because more natural settings can provide students with important motivations and feedback for learning.

You can expand and adapt a student's communication system to the natural environment in several ways. You could show a student how to use his system in a new context or activity. You could introduce a new communication partner. You could add new content to the system so that a child participates more frequently in a variety of school activities. The level of assistance provided to the student might also be reduced. Ultimately, the goal is for a student to independently access an augmentative communication device or communication system of choice and utilize the power of the device or system to establish communication with as many communication partners as possible.

Quick-Guides to Inclusion 2: Ideas for Educating Students with Disabilities © 1998 Michael F. Giangreco
Available through Paul H. Brookes Publishing Co., Baltimore: 1-800-638-3775

#8

Avoid Becoming
Overly Dependent
on High-Technology Devices

Avoid Becoming Overly Dependent on High-Technology Devices

High-technology devices have many positive features that make them attractive options for certain students. Some of these notable features include voice, print, or braille output; reprogramming capability; portability; expandability; large capacity; and switch activation (e.g., by pressing or touching the switch with any controllable body part, by tilting a mercury switch, by coming close to a magnetic or temperature-sensitive switch, by sipping or puffing on a pneumatic switch, by moving a light beam on a head switch). In today's computer-saturated society, however, it is important to remember that although high-technology AAC systems offer highly desirable features and are getting easier to use all the time, they may not be right for every student who uses AAC.

With high-technology equipment come correspondingly high-technology problems. Team members must become well-versed in troubleshooting in case something goes wrong—and it will. We don't want to discourage you from getting involved with high-technology AAC systems, but you should understand that there are limitations for which advance planning is essential. Often replacement parts can be costly, and the time needed to repair a broken device can be extensive. Many AAC users cannot afford a second high-technology back-up system. When their primary systems fail, however, they still need to communicate.

Overreliance on technology for communication can thus leave high-technology AAC users without a viable means of communication, so it is essential to have inexpensive alternatives such as low-technology AAC systems that can be put in place quickly as a temporary measure. Back-up systems should be ready for use before a high-technology breakdown occurs. If your student uses a high-technology AAC device, ask the speech-language pathologist or special educator whether a back-up system is in place so you can learn about it or so one can be developed.

Quick-Guides to Inclusion 2: Ideas for Educating Students with Disabilities   © 1998 Michael F. Giangreco
Available through Paul H. Brookes Publishing Co., Baltimore: 1-800-638-3775

#9

Update
Communication Systems
Frequently

Update Communication Systems Frequently

Communication systems are dynamic in nature and need to be expanded and modified over time. The needs and interests of students continually change (e.g., topics of interest, classes, friends, current events, hopes, dreams, experiences); therefore, the AAC system must change accordingly. AAC systems can be expanded so a student can engage in a variety of communicative functions such as greeting people, making requests, making choices, answering or asking questions, saying "yes" or "no," describing objects, commenting, relating experiences, offering opinions, expressing emotions, and conversing.

As a student gets older, the symbol choices and styles should match the student's chronological age and incorporate local slang or popular phrases. Also, the symbols should reflect the personality, cultural traditions, and perspective of the student. If the student's team does not attend to these concerns, there is the danger that the symbol system will more closely reflect the communication preferences of adult members of the team rather than those of the student.

You and other adults may have to offer support during the process of updating the AAC system. Updating may also require the student to learn new skills (e.g., expand symbol repertoire). In most cases support is provided by others at the same time that the student learns new skills. If a student makes extremely good progress with one type of symbol system, she may need to switch to a more sophisticated system. For example, systems that use pictures or drawings offer a limited number of possible messages, depending on the availability and quantity of the symbols, whereas systems based on the alphabet provide the greatest degree of communicative freedom. With an alphabet-based AAC system, the possible message combinations are limitless. Often updates and expansion include both the alphabet and word signs or symbols such as communication boards that include the alphabet plus commonly used words.

Quick-Guides to Inclusion 2: Ideas for Educating Students with Disabilities   © 1998 Michael F. Giangreco
Available through Paul H. Brookes Publishing Co., Baltimore: 1-800-638-3775

#10

Evaluate Communication Progress

Evaluate Communication Progress

Whichever communication system is selected for a student, it is important that you and other team members systematically evaluate the impact of the AAC intervention program and the student's communication progress across a variety of situations. Following are 10 questions to ask when evaluating the AAC system:

1. How often does the student access the communication system?
2. In what contexts does the student use the communication system?
3. When does the student experience the most successful communication attempts?
4. What is the student and his or her peers' interest in utilizing the communication system in academic and social contexts?
5. What other systems of communication does the student use, and how effective are these systems?
6. What is the classroom teacher's level of involvement in helping the student improve his or her communication abilities?
7. How is the curriculum adapted for and integrated into the student's augmentative communication system?
8. In which situations has communication failed between the student and his or her peers when using the communication system?
9. Which are the most effective supports currently being used to ensure communication success?
10. What are the perceptions of teachers, peers, and the student regarding the effectiveness of the communication progress?

You can use ongoing evaluation to monitor student progress and teaching effectiveness. Most important, evaluation is a tool that you can use to determine the impact of communication on a student's life.

Quick-Guides to Inclusion 2: Ideas for Educating Students with Disabilities   © 1998 Michael F. Giangreco
Available through Paul H. Brookes Publishing Co., Baltimore: 1-800-638-3775

Selected References

Baumgart, D., Johnson, J., & Helmstetter, E. (1990). *Augmentative and alternative communication systems for persons with moderate and severe disabilities.* Baltimore: Paul H. Brookes Publishing Co.

Beukelman, D.R., & Mirenda, P. (1998). *Augmentative and alternative communication: Management of severe communication disorders in children and adults* (2nd ed.). Baltimore: Paul H. Brookes Publishing Co.

Donnellan, A. (1984). The criterion of the least dangerous assumption. *Behavior Disorders, 9,* 141–150.

Johnson, J.M., Baumgart, D., Helmstetter, E., & Curry, C.A. (1996). *Augmenting basic communication in natural contexts.* Baltimore: Paul H. Brookes Publishing Co.

Lloyd, L., & Blischak, D. (1992). AAC terminology policy and issues update. *Augmentative and Alternative Communication, 8,* 104–109.

Musslewhite, C., & King-DeBaun, P. (1997). *Emergent literacy success: Merging technology and whole language for students with special needs.* Birmingham, AL: Southeast Augmentative Communication Conference Publications.

Silverman, F.H. (1995). *Communication for the speechless.* Needham Heights, MA: Allyn & Bacon.

Quick-Guide #9

Administration in Inclusive Schools

Richard Schattman and Ruth E. Dennis

Quick-Guides to Inclusion 2: Ideas for Educating Students with Disabilities

Michael F. Giangreco, Ph.D.
Series Editor

Quick-Guides to Inclusion 2: Ideas for Educating Students with Disabilities   © 1998 Michael F. Giangreco
Available through Paul H. Brookes Publishing Co., Baltimore: 1-800-638-3775

Dear School Leader,

Your board of education has just announced a plan that includes the transfer of all children with special educational needs from specialized, segregated facilities to their neighborhood schools. Because the implementation of this change will have to occur school by school, your challenge is to put together the plan for your school. You already serve students with disabilities, but this will change the scope of what your school does. You probably suspect it will be a difficult task, but it's one that hopefully excites you as you begin to envision a school that can meet the needs of all children regardless of their characteristics.

As your thoughts progress, you may realize that the changes to support full inclusion have far-reaching implications for everyone in your school and your community. The inclusion of children with significant special educational needs does not involve merely a change in student placement. Inclusion requires a comprehensive look at your community's values and beliefs regarding diversity. You will need to reexamine many of the policies and practices that have been part of the traditional structure of your school.

Creating an inclusive school challenges us to consider our core values, the efficacy of our practices, and many aspects of our daily operations. These guidelines are designed to support you as you consider ways to implement inclusive education. We realize that comprehensive school reform is needed to implement inclusive schooling, and reform never happens without some bumps in the road. Rest assured that administrators in many schools have faced this challenge and have helped develop better learning environments for all children. We hope these notes and ideas lend support to your efforts as you create a school that cares for all of its community's children.

Good Luck!

Richard and Ruth

1. Develop Shared Vision, Mission, and Belief Statements to Guide Your Efforts

2. Share Leadership Responsibilities

3. Involve Parents

4. Provide More Time to Collaborate

5. Coordinate with Other Organizations

6. Create One Tent for All Students, Parents, and Teachers

7. Create the Expectation that Every Student Takes Part in All School Activities

8. Start Early

9. Help Your School Become a Learning Organization

10. Use Performance Data to Improve Teaching and Learning

Quick-Guides to Inclusion 2: Ideas for Educating Students with Disabilities © 1998 Michael F. Giangreco
Available through Paul H. Brookes Publishing Co., Baltimore: 1-800-638-3775

#1

Develop Shared Vision, Mission, and Belief Statements to Guide Your Efforts

---

Develop Shared Vision, Mission, and Belief Statements to Guide Your Efforts

The term **strategic plan** is quite familiar to school administrators. A strategic plan is an orchestrated set of actions that are consistent with an identified vision, mission, and set of beliefs. A sound strategic plan is one key factor that differentiates schools that embrace inclusion as an essential part of education from those that view it as a "program" or practice inclusion because others say that the school "must."

Strategic plans should reflect a broad consensus among a school's constituencies. Internal constituents include teachers, support services staff, parents of attending children (both with and without disabilities), paraprofessionals, custodians, cafeteria workers, school board members, and administrators. External constituents include members of students' extended families, business leaders, civic leaders, and other interested community members.

Community Conversations is a grassroots strategy for building a unified vision (Senge, 1990). These conversations begin with broad questions such as "What is good for our children?" and "What is good for our community?" By facilitating conversations, administrators can ensure that members of the community contribute their perspectives and expand on each others' ideas so that the vision that emerges includes the concerns and interests of all children and their families.

Mission and belief statements grow out of the community's vision for the school. The mission statement reflects a realistic assessment of what influence and impact schools can have in promoting the community's vision. Belief statements about what is important to a school community serve as guiding principles by which schools make plans and assess their efforts. Administrators play a key role in ensuring that these statements of organizational integrity are validated by the school's various constituent groups, discussed, and considered on a daily basis and that school policies and practices reflect these statements.

Quick-Guides to Inclusion 2: Ideas for Educating Students with Disabilities   © 1998 Michael F. Giangreco
Available through Paul H. Brookes Publishing Co., Baltimore: 1-800-638-3775

#2

Share
Leadership
Responsibilities

Share Leadership Responsibilities

In inclusive schools, decisions that were once relegated to a few special educators are now the responsibility of general educators and principals. Educators can address the diverse needs of all children only if leadership is distributed and shared among those who have a stake in its outcomes.

Shared leadership requires administrators to foster at least three levels of teamwork. First, at the level of individual students' education teams, the role of each team member should be negotiated with other members, including parents. Administrators may support the work of the team by providing information, solving logistical problems, interpreting regulations and policies, or helping to coordinate plans with other school staff.

Second, administrators also play a role in formulating and supporting schoolwide efforts such as task force investigations on specific school priorities. These teams may address topics such as literacy, standards, curriculum, assessment, or technology. These teams articulate goals, formulate plans of action, identify needed resources, and make decisions that will have an impact on the implementation of new practices.

Finally, the administrator has a role as a member of a central administrative team. This team includes representatives from all of the various constituent groups and is primarily charged with ensuring that all of the activities of the school district align with its overall vision and mission. Through this team's work, administrators can ensure that the initiatives that will shape their school's future are coordinated with the entire school community and reflect its fundamental values and beliefs. Shared leadership requires that administrators evolve from acting as directors to encouraging leadership in others.

Quick-Guides to Inclusion 2: Ideas for Educating Students with Disabilities   © 1998 Michael F. Giangreco
Available through Paul H. Brookes Publishing Co., Baltimore: 1-800-638-3775

#3

Involve Parents

Involve Parents

Involving parents is an essential aspect of inclusive schooling. The nature of that involvement varies from school to school depending on the extent to which families perceive that they are valued members of the school community. Inviting the involvement of parents who have previously been less involved requires expanding traditional involvement opportunities in ways that are sensitive to family needs.

Each school must communicate to parents that parents play an essential role in the education of their children. Parents know their own children best, have the greatest vested interest in their outcomes, and bring valuable knowledge to the team. Therefore, families deserve to have a role in defining the school's overall vision and mission. Schools should invite all parents to contribute their perspectives and to learn from the views of others. While doing so, the school has a responsibility to recognize that all families are unique and to provide them with the support they need to articulate their concerns and priorities for their children.

As schools chart the waters of change in programs and services, parents should participate in making innovations. Many parents have the time, interest, experience, and ability to contribute to major school initiatives. Their involvement brings new information and a broader range of perspectives to the process, provides an opportunity for parents to work with the school on a proactive level, introduces parents to the school organization, and encourages investment in initiatives that have an impact on all children.

Finally, schools benefit from parent involvement when parents are elected to the board of education or when they form informal community networks. Such networks provide administrators with timely feedback on a variety of issues and topics.

Quick-Guides to Inclusion 2: Ideas for Educating Students with Disabilities   © 1998 Michael F. Giangreco
Available through Paul H. Brookes Publishing Co., Baltimore: 1-800-638-3775

#4

Provide More
Time to Collaborate

Quick-Guides to Inclusion 2: Ideas for Educating Students with Disabilities   © 1998 Michael F. Giangreco
Available through Paul H. Brookes Publishing Co., Baltimore: 1-800-638-3775

Provide More Time to Collaborate

Administrators have a responsibility to ensure that school staff have the resources they need to do their jobs effectively. One of the most critical resources in an inclusive school is time, which is necessary for collaboration among teachers, parents, related services providers, paraprofessionals, and administrators.

A number of systemic changes may be required to reallocate time for collaboration. You can consider implementing block scheduling, common planning times, and a variety of new class arrangements. In addition, innovative classroom arrangements such as loops, multi-age, and multigrade classes can maximize the efficiency of collaboration by reducing the amount of changes in team membership from year to year. It is necessary for teachers to participate in the development of the school's master schedule so they can be sure that they have the time needed to plan for all of the children in their classes.

Once time for planning becomes a part of the typical school day, teachers need to hone their meeting skills. Each meeting should be guided by an agenda that includes items important to each of the team members. Starting and stopping times should be adhered to, and a specific amount of time should be targeted for each agenda item. Accurate minutes ensure timely communication with members who may not be present. Meetings can be kept brief through the use of subteam meetings that are attended only by essential team members and that address specific issues.

As team members acquire more collaborative skills, often they come to value the opportunity to work more closely with each other. Collaborative teamwork supported by creative and efficient approaches to time utilization is an essential aspect of an inclusive school climate.

Quick-Guides to Inclusion 2: Ideas for Educating Students with Disabilities   © 1998 Michael F. Giangreco
Available through Paul H. Brookes Publishing Co., Baltimore: 1-800-638-3775

#5

Coordinate
with Other Organizations

Coordinate with Other Organizations

It is essential that inclusive schools coordinate their efforts with families and other community organizations to address the needs of children. Many social and economic factors have a significant impact on the kind of supports parents need in order to care for their children. Community members often expect schools to provide psychological nurturance, after-school programs, health and safety information, and moral guidance for children. At the same time, taxpayers, parents, and community members increasingly ask schools to account for student progress toward national and state academic standards.

As a result, schools must enter into collaborative partnerships with other organizations. A variety of sources can provide natural supports for families, such as places of worship, extended family members, child care centers, and big brother/big sister programs. Schools can forge other, more formal relationships with health and social services agencies. Agreements with agencies often include a coordinated services plan. This written agreement defines the need for the plan, desired outcomes, people's responsibilities, and time lines for specific activities. At the center of any service plan is the family, and the plan should focus on the family's goals and dreams for the future.

Contracted services also provide a mechanism for schools and community groups to link themselves to one another. The school may make a contract with its community mental health agency for the provision of intensive home-based services or may make a contract with the state or county health department for the provision of immunization clinics at school. Formal partnerships often require administrative support and sometimes policy initiatives to ensure coordinated efforts on the behalf of children.

When schools form stronger links with other community services, school personnel, families, and community groups move away from the mind-set that resources are inadequate and difficult to acquire, and they see the abundance of resources that are available for the support of their children. When this shift in viewpoint occurs, participants engage in more creative problem solving and planning.

Quick-Guides to Inclusion 2: Ideas for Educating Students with Disabilities © 1998 Michael F. Giangreco
Available through Paul H. Brookes Publishing Co., Baltimore: 1-800-638-3775

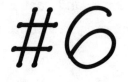

#6

Create One Tent
for All Students,
Parents, and Teachers

Quick-Guides to Inclusion 2: Ideas for Educating Students with Disabilities   © 1998 Michael F. Giangreco
Available through Paul H. Brookes Publishing Co., Baltimore: 1-800-638-3775

Create One Tent for All
Students, Parents, and Teachers

Although educators have discussed inclusive schooling for many years, high-quality inclusion is not the norm. Effective inclusion is not more common, in part, because most schools continue to operate a dual system of special and general education with organizational models and funding formulas that maintain the separation between the two types of education. In contrast, educating under **One Tent** implies that the school is for **all** children in a community. Although this idea sounds uncomplicated, it is not. This notion requires us to examine our personal beliefs about the structure of education in a democratic society and about how we operate public schools.

Under One Tent, all children receive access to necessary resources, all are held accountable to the standards that the school community has adopted, all are assessed according to those standards, and all are expected to live within established guidelines for student conduct. Such high expectations for the achievement and social development of all students should not be confused, however, with the rigid standardization of their educational experiences; One Tent does not mean "one size fits all."

Under One Tent, a special education teacher might team-teach with general educators to instruct students with and without disabilities. A special education administrator can act as a partner with the school principal. School principals can give the same responsibilities, such as supporting staff development and conducting performance evaluations, to special education staff that they give to general education staff. Central office personnel can offer their support in this process by providing technical assistance, seeking additional resources and funding, and coordinating services.

Creating One Tent for all students, parents, and teachers is a notion that is easy to understand but is somewhat more difficult to implement. It necessitates change away from practices that reflect "business as usual." Despite the changes that educating under One Tent implies, this approach to schooling is absolutely necessary if inclusive education is to become a genuine practice.

Quick-Guides to Inclusion 2: Ideas for Educating Students with Disabilities © 1998 Michael F. Giangreco
Available through Paul H. Brookes Publishing Co., Baltimore: 1-800-638-3775

#7

Create the Expectation that Every Student Takes Part in All School Activities

---

Create the Expectation that Every Student Takes Part in All School Activities

In an inclusive school, every event and activity should reflect the assumption that all children are valued and that all should have opportunities to participate. Opportunities for children with disabilities should be consistent with those available to peers without disabilities. All students should participate in core classroom activities, cocurricular units, community activities, and special school events. Some students may require individualized supports or adaptations to participate.

Administrators devote much of their attention to supporting student instruction in the classroom. In order to address ways of making education meaningful for all students, you must extend your thinking to the cocurricular and extracurricular areas that account for much of the enrichment and extension of classroom learning. Rather than assuming that assigning a paraprofessional to a student will satisfy a student's support needs, you must look toward increasing the capacity of classroom teachers, coaches, club leaders, and peers as natural supports.

Administrators should also address behavioral expectations for participation. Schools that have thoughtful, supportive, and clear expectations for student behavior should apply those standards fairly to all students while accounting for individual differences. Students who display challenging behaviors should receive appropriate supports; regardless of whether they have a disability, however, they cannot be allowed to disrupt the learning of their classmates. Obviously, schools must take care to support and teach rather than punish and exclude students who exhibit challenging behaviors. An administrator can be crucial in identifying the nature and source of supports that a teacher needs to help an individual student to participate, including classroom management strategies, peer supports, cooperative groupings, or development of crisis intervention plans of action.

Quick-Guides to Inclusion 2: Ideas for Educating Students with Disabilities   © 1998 Michael F. Giangreco
Available through Paul H. Brookes Publishing Co., Baltimore: 1-800-638-3775

#8

Start Early

Start Early

An inclusive school has a vested interest in ensuring that 1) children enter school with foundations to support early learning; 2) education programs are ready to meet children's needs; and 3) parents are interested, knowledgeable, and involved in their children's education. High-quality early intervention programs are critically important to schools and communities for several reasons. First, the programs can identify and minimize critical developmental needs at a time when they first become evident. The challenge of including children with special needs in general classrooms in later school years is diminished when their needs are identified and addressed early. Second, early intervention and preschool special education services attend to both the skills that children need to develop and those that teachers must have to prepare children for success in future environments such as kindergarten. Transition activities are critical when planning to include children with disabilities in the general classroom, a process that was once called "mainstreaming." Finally, early intervention programs have the opportunity to support families who advocate for their children's integrated educational program in positive and productive ways.

Both schools and early intervention programs can improve the support they offer by making deliberate efforts to locate early childhood service providers in physical proximity to, and preferably within, the school itself. Proximity affords parents the opportunity to meet and become familiar with other parents and future teachers, helps early childhood and school staff to share knowledge and other resources, allows parents and children to explore future environments and routines (e.g., the library, lunch in the cafeteria), and lets children become comfortable in "their school" before they enter kindergarten.

Starting early reflects a proactive culture within a school and shows that the school values planning, preparation, and forethought. These elements are essential as schools provide high-quality, caring inclusive education to young children.

Quick-Guides to Inclusion 2: Ideas for Educating Students with Disabilities   © 1998 Michael F. Giangreco
Available through Paul H. Brookes Publishing Co., Baltimore: 1-800-638-3775

#9

Help Your School Become
a Learning Organization

Quick-Guides to Inclusion 2: Ideas for Educating Students with Disabilities   © 1998 Michael F. Giangreco
Available through Paul H. Brookes Publishing Co., Baltimore: 1-800-638-3775

106

Professionals on an education team must have a supportive network from which to derive motivation, energy, and a feeling of success. In inclusive schools, the professional community is enlarged when the school becomes a **learning organization** that includes professionals across disciplines and their community of consumers. New ideas and approaches emerge from this community. The learning organization assumes responsibility for planning professional development, and members often look to each other for new information or mentoring.

Schools that are learning organizations possess a number of important qualities. First, they welcome critical review and input from various stakeholder groups, including teachers, administrators, parents, support staff, and other community members. Second, learning organizations demonstrate a commitment to teamwork based on trust and shared goals. This willingness to embrace a team approach reduces professional isolation often experienced by those operating in more traditional professional arenas. Third, learning organizations examine problems and seek support and solutions in creative ways. They are willing to take risks and implement innovative practices because they know that they can learn from their mistakes as well as from their successes. Fourth, learning organizations reflect on the content and process of their work simultaneously to develop standards of professional practice that are more inclusive and community based and that improve morale among staff.

Finally, learning organizations attend to their own need for renewal. Renewal occurs through staff development as well as activities of recognition. Staff meetings might be punctuated by ceremonies of recognition for a job well done or a shared victory. Although learning organizations value teamwork, they can also recognize and celebrate individual achievement.

Quick-Guides to Inclusion 2: Ideas for Educating Students with Disabilities   © 1998 Michael F. Giangreco
Available through Paul H. Brookes Publishing Co., Baltimore: 1-800-638-3775

#10

Use Performance
Data to Improve
Teaching and Learning

Use Performance Data to Improve Teaching and Learning

Historically, community leaders, parents, legislators, and state departments of education have asked schools to provide student performance data based on standardized achievement tests. Some educators view this as a reason to exclude students with disabilities from testing for fear that they will lower score averages. Only when we are willing to let our student assessments reflect the performance of **all** children will public education systems gain a comprehensive portrait of the strengths and needs of schools. Inclusive schools extend this narrow view of outcomes and performance measurement by using authentic assessment such as standards-based assessment, portfolios, or alternative portfolios.

To collect performance data for all children, some schools will need to make accommodations in assessment strategies (e.g., by extending time limits, by providing large-print material). These accommodations may make it more difficult for individual schools and school systems to use data in traditional ways, such as by making quantitative comparisons among schools. Instead, data that reflects accommodations for students with special needs can be used to describe changes within a school over time.

The inclusion of students with disabilities as part of comprehensive student assessment can stimulate a broad range of initiatives that will benefit the entire school. Results of assessments that include all students, for example, can help teachers identify professional development goals. This encourages teachers to evaluate how they can best instruct all of the children in their classrooms. In an inclusive school, such teacher evaluation provides an opportunity for teachers to gain insights and support for their efforts to address diverse student needs in the classroom. This type of staff evaluation can be applied to other professional staff including special educators and related services providers. Principals and other school leaders model their commitment to a truly inclusive system by taking responsibility for evaluating all staff as a group working together toward a common goal.

Quick-Guides to Inclusion 2: Ideas for Educating Students with Disabilities © 1998 Michael F. Giangreco
Available through Paul H. Brookes Publishing Co., Baltimore: 1-800-638-3775

Selected References

Hilliard, A. (1991). Do we have the will to educate all children? *Educational Leadership, 9*, 31–35.

Noddings, N. (1995). A morally defensible mission for schools in the 21st century. *Phi Delta Kappan, 76*(5), 365–368.

Pugach, M.C. (1990). The moral cost of retrenchment in special education. *Journal of Special Education, 24*(3), 326–333.

Roach, V. (1995). Supporting inclusion: Beyond the rhetoric. *Phi Delta Kappan, 77*(4), 295–299.

Sarason, S.B. (1995). *Parental involvement and the political principal: Why existing structures of schools should be abolished.* San Francisco: Jossey-Bass.

Schattman, R., & Pearo, L. (1996). One school's journey to full inclusion. *IMPACT (Institute on Community Integration, University of Minnesota), 9*(2), 12–13.

Seely, D.S. (1989). A new paradigm for parent involvement. *Educational Leadership, 47*(2), 46–48.

Senge, P. (1990). *The fifth discipline: The art and practice of the learning organization.* New York: Doubleday/Currency.

Skrtic, T.M. (1991). The special education paradox: Equity as the way to excellence. *Harvard Education Review, 61*(2), 148–206

Tusnhet, N. (1993). *A guide to developing educational partnerships.* Washington, DC: U.S. Department of Education.

Villa, R.A., Thousand, J.S., Stainback, W., & Stainback S. (1992). *Restructuring for caring and effective education: An administrative guide to creating heterogeneous schools.* Baltimore: Paul H. Brookes Publishing Co.

Quick-Guides to Inclusion 2: Ideas for Educating Students with Disabilities © 1998 Michael F. Giangreco
Available through Paul H. Brookes Publishing Co., Baltimore: 1-800-638-3775

Quick-Guide #10

Transition from School to Adult Life

George B. Salembier and Katharine S. Furney

Quick-Guides to Inclusion 2:
Ideas for Educating Students with Disabilities

Michael F. Giangreco, Ph.D.
Series Editor

Quick-Guides to Inclusion 2: Ideas for Educating Students with Disabilities © 1998 Michael F. Giangreco
Available through Paul H. Brookes Publishing Co., Baltimore: 1-800-638-3775

Dear Teacher,

Have you ever wondered what happens to your students with disabilities once they leave high school? Unfortunately, national studies show that without adequate supports, these former students may find themselves unemployed or underemployed, without access to postsecondary education and vocational training, and lacking connections to the community. To promote more positive adult life outcomes for students with disabilities, the federal government added a transition services requirement to the 1990 reauthorization of the Individuals with Disabilities Education Act (IDEA) (PL 101-476). This requirement, retained in the 1997 version of IDEA (PL 105-17), specifies that the individualized education programs (IEPs) developed for students with disabilities must contain goals and activities to help them achieve a successful transition from school to adult life.

This Quick-Guide suggests guidelines that you may use to ensure that students with disabilities have the opportunities, options, and supports they need to advocate for themselves and to make a successful transition from school to adult life. Each guideline includes a brief description and examples of ways to make transition planning more student and family centered, collaborative, and effective. We hope these guidelines will assist you and the students and families with whom you work in facilitating successful transitions to adult life.

Good Luck!

George and Katie

1. Plan Early

2. Build a Strong Team Around the Student

3. Make Sure Transition Planning Is Student and Family Centered

4. Encourage Students to Advocate for Themselves

5. Develop Plans Based on Students' Strengths, Dreams, and Needs

6. Connect Transition Goals to Other Goals in Your Student's IEP

7. Help Students Draw on a Range of School and Community Resources

8. Build a Strong Network of Support in the Community

9. Review the Plan at Least Once a Year

10. Remember that Transition Planning Benefits All Students

Quick-Guides to Inclusion 2: Ideas for Educating Students with Disabilities © 1998 Michael F. Giangreco
Available through Paul H. Brookes Publishing Co., Baltimore: 1-800-638-3775

#1

Plan Early

Plan Early

IDEA '97 states that the IEPs of students with disabilities ages 14 and older must include a statement of transition services needs and that the IEPs of students 16 years of age and older must specify the types of transition services needed by the student as well as a plan for implementing these services. Early planning is important for several reasons.

First, early planning allows you and other team members to become aware of a student's postschool goals related to employment, postsecondary education, independent living, and community participation. The education team should use these goals as the basis for identifying the courses and experiences a student should have while in high school. Students who do not have a clear idea about what they would like to do after high school will thus have time to explore possibilities in their school and community, and their experiences may help them establish personal goals for the future.

Second, early planning allows students and their families to learn about community resources and supports that are available both during and after high school. Many of these resources have eligibility requirements and waiting lists that students and their families need to know about.

Third, early planning allows team members to identify representatives from adult services or postsecondary education institutions that should be invited to attend future team meetings and/or to become team members. Finally, students and their families need plenty of time to make informed choices about the future and to learn how to advocate for themselves in their schools and communities.

Quick-Guides to Inclusion 2: Ideas for Educating Students with Disabilities   © 1998 Michael F. Giangreco
Available through Paul H. Brookes Publishing Co., Baltimore: 1-800-638-3775

#2

Build a Strong Team
Around the Student

Build a Strong Team Around the Student

Prior to the first meeting in which transition planning will be discussed, you will need to identify people who will be members of the student's transition team and IEP team. According to IDEA '97, the transition team must consist of the student, her IEP team, and any adult services representatives who may provide future services to the student. The transition team must meet annually to review the student's transition plan but may meet more frequently to review progress being made on specific goals and activities.

IDEA '97 defines the **IEP team** as the student's parents, at least one general education teacher, at least one special education teacher, a representative from the local education agency (LEA) who is knowledgeable about curriculum and availability of resources, and an individual who can interpret evaluation results. At the discretion of the parents or the LEA representative, the IEP team may also include other individuals familiar with the student, including related services providers. In addition, it may be helpful to include individuals who are not IEP team members but who may be interested in assisting the student in transition planning. These individuals might include siblings, friends, grandparents, or other community members who can provide unique perspectives on the student and can provide links to employment, living situations, and recreational opportunities.

As you consider team membership, it is important to weigh the pros and cons of large and small teams. Larger teams may provide you with more ideas and perspectives, but they may also become difficult to manage. You may wish to consider differentiating between team members who need to attend all transition-planning meetings and those who should be invited only to selected meetings for specific purposes. For example, a student's current employer does not need to attend all transition-planning meetings, but you might want to invite him to attend an annual review at which employment goals will be discussed.

Quick-Guides to Inclusion 2: Ideas for Educating Students with Disabilities   © 1998 Michael F. Giangreco
Available through Paul H. Brookes Publishing Co., Baltimore: 1-800-638-3775

#3

Make Sure Transition Planning Is Student and Family Centered

Make Sure Transition Planning Is Student and Family Centered

In order for students to become participating members of their schools and communities, the transition-planning process needs to be student and family centered. By this, we mean that the transition-planning process should be directed by students and family members and built on their ideas about what is most important in the student's life. As a teacher, you can help to ensure that transition planning is student and family centered by encouraging teams to use one of a number of specific planning processes that are designed to support students and families in expressing and clarifying their vision for the student's future. Examples of these processes include Choosing Outcomes and Accommodations for Children (COACH) (Giangreco, Cloninger, & Iverson, 1998), Making Action Plans (MAPs) (Pearpoint, Forest, & O'Brien, 1996), and Planning Alternative Tomorrows with Hope (PATH) (Pearpoint, O'Brien, & Forest, 1993). These processes stress the importance of building strong relationships and good communication with students and families before, during, and after all transition-planning meetings.

Before the annual transition-planning meetings occur, it is important for the rest of the transition team to make sure that students and family members understand the purpose of the meetings and that they understand their legal rights and responsibilities. Students and family members should be involved in choosing the composition of the IEP teams and transition teams, the times and places of meetings, and meeting agendas. During transition-planning meetings, try to encourage student and parent participation by using active listening skills, by directing questions to students and parents, and by conveying a sense that you care about and are open to acting on what they want for the future. After meetings, you can continue to include students and parents by touching base with them regularly, sharing information, and continuing to build a strong and ongoing relationship.

Quick-Guides to Inclusion 2: Ideas for Educating Students with Disabilities   © 1998 Michael F. Giangreco
Available through Paul H. Brookes Publishing Co., Baltimore: 1-800-638-3775

#4

Encourage Students to Advocate for Themselves

Encourage Students to Advocate for Themselves

An important aspect of making transition planning a student- and family-centered process is encouraging students to advocate for themselves during planning meetings and in their daily lives. Self-advocacy has been defined as an individual's ability to identify his personal needs and preferences, express those needs to others, make informed choices, and take responsibility for the outcomes of his actions (Abery et al., 1994; Sands & Wehmeyer, 1996). You can use the transition-planning process as an opportunity to encourage self-advocacy among students by involving them in preparing for their transition-planning meetings.

You may find it helpful to talk with students before meetings about the kinds of questions that may be asked and to help them prepare their own responses, questions, and comments. During each meeting, you should ask your student to respond to questions concerning her before you invite others to respond, encourage your student to share previously prepared notes, and invite her to assume responsibility for carrying out specific activities on her IEP and transition plan. You can also foster self-advocacy by creating a comfortable and relaxed atmosphere and by encouraging the student to invite her friends to meetings.

Outside of the planning meetings, you can promote self-advocacy by providing the student with various opportunities to make choices about her course of studies, extracurricular activities, and recreational activities and by encouraging her to express her needs in appropriate ways. Many students benefit from instruction in specific self-advocacy skills such as self-assessment, goal setting, problem solving, communicating, and resolving conflicts. It is important to remember that self-advocacy means different things to different people and should be considered within the context of a student's age, culture, and degree of support needs.

Quick-Guides to Inclusion 2: Ideas for Educating Students with Disabilities   © 1998 Michael F. Giangreco
Available through Paul H. Brookes Publishing Co., Baltimore: 1-800-638-3775

#5

Develop Plans Based on Students' Strengths, Dreams, and Needs

---

Develop Plans Based on
Students' Strengths, Dreams, and Needs

The student's current strengths, dreams for the future, and needs provide the building blocks for his IEP and transition plan. In the context of transition planning, **strengths** refer to a student's personal qualities, skills, interests, and preferences. The person-centered processes mentioned in Guideline #3 (i.e., COACH, MAPs, PATH) use a strengths-based approach to planning. This strengths-based approach is an alternative to traditional models of planning and assessment, which tend to focus on identifying students' areas of weakness in an effort to remediate them and teach new skills. Strengths-based planning focuses on what a student **can** do rather than on what he cannot do. **Dreams** refer to what a student wants to achieve both during and after high school. Dreams may be related to his chosen course of study, employment, postsecondary education or vocational training, independent living, health, relationships, community participation, or personal interests. **Needs** refer to the skills and opportunities that a student requires in order to live in the community and wishes to acquire in order to pursue his dreams. Once again, it is important to think about a student's needs in terms of strengths rather than weaknesses.

Often, students have not had many opportunities to talk about their strengths, dreams, and needs, so it is important to prepare them to do this before their transition-planning meetings. During each meeting, invite the student, her parents, and other team members to brainstorm and answer specific questions about the student's strengths, dreams, and needs. This information will be used later to identify goals, activities, and resources to be included in the student's IEP and transition plan.

Quick-Guides to Inclusion 2: Ideas for Educating Students with Disabilities   © 1998 Michael F. Giangreco
Available through Paul H. Brookes Publishing Co., Baltimore: 1-800-638-3775

#6

Connect Transition Goals
to Other Goals
in Your Student's IEP

Connect Transition Goals to Other Goals in Your Student's IEP

Once IEP and transition teams have identified strengths, dreams, and needs, they need to translate them into goals, objectives, services, and activities that will make up yearly IEPs and transition plans. One way to accomplish this is to develop a list of long-range transition goals that articulate the student's dreams related to the areas of employment, post-secondary or vocational education, independent living, health, relationships, community participation, or personal interests. Next, you and the rest of the IEP and transition team should decide what needs to occur in the coming year in order to move the student closer to his long-term transition goals. The IEP team can then use these decisions to inform and identify annual IEP goals and related transition activities that are appropriate for the student.

In addition, the team needs to consider the student's transition goals when designing his general course of studies. For example, imagine that a student with learning disabilities named George has told you that he wants to help build houses and plans to attend a technical school after high school to acquire additional skills. His IEP goals and objectives might be related to improving organizational skills; extending reading skills; learning geometry, calculation, and measurement; and preparing job applications. His course of study during high school should include courses required for admission to technical college and technical education classes in his area of interest. In addition, George might benefit from some work-based opportunities such as job shadowing on a construction site and an apprenticeship with contractors and carpenters in his community.

It is important to remember that **all** educational goals, activities, and services should support a student's progress toward his transition goals and dreams. In other words, his dreams and long-term transition goals should provide the focus through which to develop his IEP, his transition plan, and the general high school curriculum.

Quick-Guides to Inclusion 2: Ideas for Educating Students with Disabilities   © 1998 Michael F. Giangreco
Available through Paul H. Brookes Publishing Co., Baltimore: 1-800-638-3775

#7

Help Students Draw
on a Range of School
and Community Resources

Help Students Draw on a Range of School and Community Resources

A number of available resources and supports help students to achieve their transition goals and become increasingly independent and connected to the community. As indicated in Guideline #6, a student's transition plan should include a variety of transition-related objectives and activities that tap into school and community resources. These might include obtaining part-time and/or summer employment, receiving training and supports related to finding and maintaining employment; participating in consumer and vocational training, obtaining a driver's license; learning how to manage finances and live independently; participating in community recreational activities; and learning about postsecondary education options, financial aid, and admissions requirements.

Some students and their families will need additional postschool supports that are provided by vocational rehabilitation, mental health, and mental retardation/developmental disabilities agencies; state employment and training departments; and centers for independent living and self-advocacy. Depending on a family's interests and needs, you might help family members to benefit from these resources by contacting the student's guidance counselor and/or special educator to obtain information, going with the family to visit a variety of agencies, and encouraging family members to attend resource fairs at your high school or local parent information center. Try contacting local parent organizations to introduce parents to other families who have used community resources, and invite agency representatives to attend transition-planning meetings as early as possible. Each of these activities will help students and families to learn about eligibility requirements, application procedures, contact people, and the nature of the available community services and supports.

Quick-Guides to Inclusion 2: Ideas for Educating Students with Disabilities   © 1998 Michael F. Giangreco
Available through Paul H. Brookes Publishing Co., Baltimore: 1-800-638-3775

#8

Build a Strong Network of
Support in the Community

Build a Strong Network
of Support in the Community

In the context of transition planning, a **network** refers to people who care about the student, live and/or work in her community, and are willing to support her during and after high school. There are a number of reasons why it is important to build a strong network of community support around students with disabilities. Students who are connected to a community network are more likely to have experiences and opportunities available to them, to obtain employment or postsecondary education on graduation, and to know both paid and unpaid people who will continue to support them in achieving their long-range goals once they have left high school. People in a student's network may also become friends who will help him to develop other friendships and to participate in recreational activities in the community.

You can help a student build a network of community support by asking community members who the student and her family know to attend IEP and transition-planning meetings to help with brainstorming ideas for possible employment, living, and/or recreational opportunities. You can also help build a student's network of support by involving community members in specific activities listed on his transition plan. You may want to encourage students to join local organizations or clubs of interest, youth or adult advocacy groups, community service groups, or groups affiliated with places of worship. The workplace is an excellent location for you to facilitate natural connections between a student and one or more co-workers. In these ways, you may teach students that they have a role to play in building community networks. You may develop this awareness further by teaching social, communication, and self-advocacy skills that will allow students to initiate interactions that may eventually lead to friendships and wider networks of support.

Quick-Guides to Inclusion 2: Ideas for Educating Students with Disabilities   © 1998 Michael F. Giangreco
Available through Paul H. Brookes Publishing Co., Baltimore: 1-800-638-3775

#9

Review the Plan
at Least Once a Year

Review the Plan at Least Once a Year

The annual review of the IEP and transition plan provides your team members with a natural opportunity to give feedback on the student's progress in achieving annual transition goals and objectives, as well as to consider whether team members need to clarify or revise the goals they developed at the outset of transition planning. This review of the student's progress in relation to postschool goals also allows team members to change the plan for the coming year. You should remind a student and her family members to be sure that goals continue to be based on her needs, preferences, and interests. The IEP and transition-planning process is a dynamic one in which the student's goals may change direction or become more focused over time.

Team membership, too, may change as the student's needs and interests shift and become clearer. To deal with these changes, it is common for teams to invite adult services providers to transition-planning meetings during the student's final 2 years of high school. You can help the annual review meeting become a time of celebration by inviting the student and other team members to tell stories of the student's accomplishments during the past year. A team member can record these stories on a large piece of flipchart paper or in a journal as part of a portfolio documenting the student's achievements. Often, reviews of the IEP and transition plan reveal unanticipated positive results. One parent told us that the end-of-year review and celebration reminded him that "our daughter is probably capable of more than we might have expected, especially in the areas of employment and independent living."

Quick-Guides to Inclusion 2: Ideas for Educating Students with Disabilities   © 1998 Michael F. Giangreco
Available through Paul H. Brookes Publishing Co., Baltimore: 1-800-638-3775

#10

Remember that Transition Planning Benefits All Students

Remember that Transition Planning Benefits All Students

As a final note, we encourage you to think of ways in which you can apply the principles and practices associated with transition planning to benefit students both with and without disabilities. A growing movement in public education stresses focusing on the school-to-adult life transition of **all** students. The federal government responded by passing the School-to-Work Opportunities Act of 1994 (PL 103-239) and by making related policies and practices in education that focus on school- and work-based learning opportunities. For example, many schools have implemented programs to provide applied learning experiences and career portfolios; service learning and community service opportunities; and employment opportunities such as apprenticeships, entrepreneurships, and internships. Usually, any student may participate in these programs and receive credit toward graduation.

You can help promote this emphasis on career and transition planning for all students by checking with your school's guidance department to find out what resources and program options are available in your school and community. Guidance counselors can play a critical role in helping all students to make a successful transition to adult life because counselors are usually responsible for helping students develop 4-year plans of study and have direct access to information on postsecondary education, training options, and career assessment opportunities. You may also wish to identify ways in which you can expand your own curriculum content and connect it to existing programs to help students attain their career goals. Educators in today's schools are beginning to realize that expanding curriculum and collaborating with the community leads to the development of a community that supports its schools and its school system.

Quick-Guides to Inclusion 2: Ideas for Educating Students with Disabilities   © 1998 Michael F. Giangreco
Available through Paul H. Brookes Publishing Co., Baltimore: 1-800-638-3775

Selected References

Abery, B., Eggebeen, A., Rudrud, L., Arndt, K., Tetu, L., Barosko, J., Hinga, A., McBride, M., Greger, P., & Peterson, K. (1994). *Self-determination for youth with disabilities: A family education curriculum.* Minneapolis: University of Minnesota, Institute on Community Integration.

Furney, K.S., Carlson, N., Lisi, D., & Yuan, S. (1993). *Speak up for yourself and your future! A curriculum for building self-advocacy and self-determination skills.* Burlington: University of Vermont, Department of Education.

Giangreco, M.F., Cloninger, C.J., & Iverson, V.S. (1998). *Choosing outcomes and accommodations for children (COACH): A guide to educational planning for students with disabilities* (2nd ed.). Baltimore: Paul H. Brookes Publishing Co.

Individuals with Disabilities Education Act (IDEA) of 1990, PL 101-476, 20 U.S.C. §§ 1400 et seq.

Individuals with Disabilities Education Act Amendments of 1997, PL 105-17, 20 U.S.C. §§ 1400 et seq.

Pearpoint, J., Forest, M., & O'Brien, J. (1996). MAPs, Circles of Friends, and PATH: Powerful tools to help build caring communities. In S. Stainback & W. Stainback (Eds.), *Inclusion: A guide for educators* (pp. 67–86). Baltimore: Paul H. Brookes Publishing Co.

Pearpoint, J., O'Brien, J., & Forest, M. (1993). *PATH.* Toronto, Ontario, Canada: Inclusion Press.

Sands, D.J., & Wehmeyer, M.L. (Eds.). (1996). *Self-determination across the life-span: Independence and choice for people with disabilities.* Baltimore: Paul H. Brookes Publishing Co.

School-to-Work Opportunities Act of 1994, PL 103-239, 20 U.S.C. §§ 6101 et seq.